OCCASIONAL PAPER 102

Financial Sector Reforms and Exchange Arrangements in Eastern Europe

Part I Financial Markets and Intermediation
By Guillermo A. Calvo and Manmohan S. Kumar

Part II Exchange Arrangements of Previously Centrally Planned Economies
By Eduardo Borensztein and Paul R. Masson

INTERNATIONAL MONETARY FUND
Washington DC
February 1993

© 1993 International Monetary Fund

Cataloging-in-Publication Data

Financial sector reforms and exchange arrangements in Eastern Europe / [two papers by Guillermo A. Calvo . . . et al.].
  p. cm. — (Occasional Paper / International Monetary Fund, ISSN 0251-6365 ; no. 102)
  Includes bibliographical references.
  Contents: Pt. 1. Financial markets and intermediation / Guillermo A. Calvo and Manmohan S. Kumar — Pt. 2. Exchange arrangements of previously centrally planned economies / Eduardo Borensztein and Paul R. Masson.
  ISBN 1-55775-279-6 : $15.00
  1. Financial institutions — Europe, Eastern. 2. Foreign exchange—Europe, Eastern. 3. Capital market — Europe, Eastern. 4. Banks and banking—Europe, Eastern. 5. Monetary policy — Europe, Eastern. 6. Privatization — Europe, Eastern. I. Calvo, Guillermo. II. Series : Occasional paper (International Monetary Fund) ; no. 102.
HG186.E82F57 1993   92-45213
332.1'0947—dc20   CIP

Price: US$15.00
(US$12.00 to full-time faculty members and
students at universities and colleges)

Please send orders to:
International Monetary Fund, Publication Services
700 19th Street, N.W., Washington, D.C. 20431, U.S.A.
Tel.: (202) 623-7430   Telefax: (202) 623-7201

recycled paper

Contents

		Page
Preface		vii

Part I **Financial Markets and Intermediation**
Guillermo A. Calvo and Manmohan S. Kumar

I.	**Introduction**	3

II.	**Recent Developments and the Role of the Financial Sector**	4
	Recent Economic Developments	4
	Role of the Financial Sector	6

III.	**Development of the Financial Sector**	7
	Prereform Financial System	7
	Reforms and the Two-Tier Banking System	7

IV.	**Performance of the Banking Sector**	13
	Quality of Loan Portfolios	13
	Enterprise Restructuring and Credit Allocation	15
	Competition in the Banking Sector	16

V.	**Privatization and Capital Markets**	17
	Equity Markets	17
	Banks and the Privatization Process	19

VI.	**Financial Sector Reforms and Stabilization Policies**	21
	Monetary Policy	21
	Fiscal Policy	23
	Exchange Rate Policy and Convertibility	24

VII.	**Credibility and Prudential Supervision**	26
	Confidence Building	26
	Deposit Protection Schemes	26

VIII.	**Summary and Conclusions**	28

                                                                            Page

**Appendix. Corporate Financing Patterns: Some Illustrative
Evidence**   29

References   32

Tables

1.   Eastern Europe: Recent Economic Developments   5
2.   Eastern Europe: Financial Sector Reforms   8
3.   Eastern Europe: Domestic Credit   11
4.   Eastern Europe: Monetary Policy   22

Appendix Tables

1.   Large Industrial Countries: Financing of Nonfinancial Enter-
         prises, 1970–85   30
2.   Selected Developing Countries: Financing of Nonfinancial
         Enterprises, 1980–88   30
3.   Selected Developing Countries: Equity Market
         Concentration   31

Charts

1.   Domestic Credit in Eastern European Countries, 1986–91   12
2.   Money Velocity in Eastern European Countries, 1986–91   23

**Part II   Exchange Arrangements of Previously Centrally Planned
Economies**

Eduardo Borensztein and Paul R. Masson

I.   Introduction   37

II.   Currency Convertibility   39
          Current Account Convertibility   39
          Capital Account Convertibility   40
          Speed of the Move to Convertibility and Preconditions for
            Its Success   40

III.   The Desirable Degree of Exchange Rate Flexibility   42
          Advantages of Exchange Rate Stability   42
          A Currency Board   43
          Implementing Exchange Rate Stability   43
          Implementing a Floating Rate   44
          Dual Exchange Rates   44
          Conclusions   45

IV.   The Experience of Eastern European Countries   46
          Convertibility   46
          Exchange Arrangements and Domestic Stabilization   47
          Exchange Arrangements and International Competitiveness   49
          CMEA Trade and Payments   53
          Lessons from the Eastern European Experience   53

V.   Summary and Conclusions   56

Page

References   57

Tables

1. Eastern Europe: Trade with CMEA and Non-CMEA Areas 48
2. Eastern Europe and the U.S.S.R.: Shares of Exports to
   Former CMEA Countries in Total Exports, 1989 54
3. Eastern Europe: Annual Changes in the Volume of
   Exports, 1991 54

Charts

1. Eastern Europe: Exchange Rates 51
2. Eastern Europe: CPI Inflation Rates 52

The following symbols have been used throughout this paper:

. . . to indicate that data are not available;

— to indicate that the figure is zero or less than half the final digit shown, or that the item does not exist;

– between years or months (e.g., 1991–92 or January–June) to indicate the years or months covered, including the beginning and ending years or months;

/ between years (e.g., 1991/92) to indicate a crop or fiscal (financial) year.

"Billion" means a thousand million.

Minor discrepancies between constituent figures and totals are due to rounding.

The term "country," as used in this paper, does not in all cases refer to a territorial entity that is a state as understood by international law and practice; the term also covers some territorial entities that are not states, but for which statistical data are maintained and provided internationally on a separate and independent basis.

Preface

The papers in this volume were originally prepared in early 1992 for discussion in the Fund's Executive Board. They deal with two of the key issues facing the economies in transition in Eastern Europe: how to develop their financial sectors along market lines and what type of exchange arrangements to adopt. The first paper discusses developments in the financial sector and constraints on the performance of recently constituted commercial banks, as well as issues related to privatization, stabilization policies, and prudential supervision. The second paper discusses the extent to which exchange arrangements in these countries have contributed to the reform process and the restructuring under way. Events may have already overtaken some of the information in this paper, reflecting the rapid changes occurring in these economies as well as the usual time lags between preparation and publication.

The authors of Part I of this Occasional Paper are indebted to Ajai Chopra, Eric Clifton, David Coe, Omotunde Johnson, Mark Stone, Nissanke Weerasinghe, and, especially, to Peter Wickham for very useful comments and suggestions on earlier drafts of the paper. They would also like to express appreciation to Marco Lari for excellent research assistance.

Part II, prepared by Eduardo Borensztein and Paul R. Masson, benefited from comments by Charles Adams, David Burton, and Bankim Chadha. The authors would like to thank Youkyong Kwon for research assistance.

The authors of both papers are grateful to David Folkerts-Landau, Timothy Lane, Donald Mathieson, and, especially, Peter Isard for their valuable comments. They would like to thank other colleagues in European I and the Policy Development and Review Department for comments and for furnishing data. Margaret Casey and Elisa Diehl of the External Relations Department edited the papers and coordinated production, and Alicia Etchebarne-Bourdin, also of the External Relations Department, provided typesetting assistance. The views expressed here, as well as any errors, are the sole responsibility of the authors and do not reflect the opinions of the IMF Executive Board or IMF staff.

Part I

Financial Markets and Intermediation

I Introduction

This paper analyzes a number of issues related to the development of financial markets in the previously centrally planned economies (PCPEs) of Eastern Europe.[1] These economies have embarked on major structural reforms to replace central planning with market mechanisms, both in the allocation of factors of production and in the production and distribution of goods and services. In most cases, they are implementing these reforms together with stabilization policies to deal with severe macroeconomic disequilibria. It is widely acknowledged that the success of the stabilization policies and the structural reforms depends in an important way on the development of efficient financial intermediaries and of credit and capital markets more generally.

The main issues concerning the development of financial markets revolve around the likely efficiency of these markets in mobilizing savings and in channeling them optimally, so as to facilitate the massive restructuring of the productive sectors that is essential for any sustained improvement in productivity and economic growth. At the same time, these markets play a critical role in facilitating transactions and in providing instruments for the conduct of monetary, fiscal, and exchange rate policies. Indeed, the implementation and efficacy of these policies depend on the efficiency of the financial markets; the role of these markets in monitoring, evaluating, and improving managerial performance can also be very important.

Although the scope and pace of financial sector reforms differ significantly among the PCPEs, they share certain characteristics, including the legacy of central planning, with severe distortions and dislocation in the financial and productive sectors; the lack of adequate financial and skilled manpower resources to develop the financial sector, as well as a lack of competition in it; the inadequacy or lack of auditing systems to provide information on the creditworthiness of prospective borrowers; underdeveloped and slow processes for settling transactions other than in cash; and the poor quality of bank portfolios and inadequate capitalization.

The paper is organized as follows: Section II provides an overview of recent developments and the role the financial sector can play, while Section III examines the development of the banking sector and contrasts the prereform system with the emerging system. Section IV focuses on some of the key weaknesses in the banking sector, including the poor quality of bank loan portfolios, inadequate capitalization, uncertain prospects of enterprises, and limited competition. Section V discusses the factors that influence the development of securities markets, in particular, the equity markets, and the role that such markets can play in privatization. Section VI discusses the conduct of monetary, fiscal, and exchange rate policies and how the emerging financial sector can affect their implementation. Section VII discusses the steps that need to be taken to establish the credibility of the new financial institutions, in particular, confidence in the banking sector, and to encourage optimal risk taking. Section VIII summarizes the major issues raised in the paper.

---

[1] It primarily addresses the development of the financial sectors in Bulgaria, Czechoslovakia, Hungary, Poland, and Romania. Several of the broader issues also apply to other PCPEs, including the states of the former Soviet Union.

II Recent Developments and the Role of the Financial Sector

This section notes recent economic developments in the Eastern European countries, in particular, the sharp declines in output and real earnings. Among the reasons for the declines were the inevitable consequences of capital stock obsolescence and inefficiencies under the planned regimes, but problems in the financial sector, which led to an inadequate provision of credit to the enterprise sector, may also have been important.

Recent Economic Developments

In 1990, real GDP declined by over 10 percent in Bulgaria and Poland, and by 4 percent and 7 percent, respectively, in Hungary and Romania (see Table 1). In all countries except Poland, the declines in output were even more pronounced in 1991 but appear to be less marked in some countries during 1992. It has been suggested that the measured output decline may overstate the actual decline owing to an increase in private sector output that is not fully measured because of index number problems resulting from rapid price changes.[2] Nevertheless, the decline in output, particularly in industrial sectors, has been substantial and greater than anticipated.

In broad terms, the output decline may be regarded partly as an inevitable consequence of capital stock obsolescence and inefficiencies under the planned regimes and partly as the result of more specific phenomena, including the collapse of the old command linkages between enterprises, which have not yet been fully replaced by the market system; the disintegration of the old incentive system; the collapse of the trading arrangements within the Council for Mutual Economic Assistance (CMEA) and changes in the terms of trade;[3] and the pursuit of requisite stabilization policies. In some countries, the provision of real credit may have been squeezed owing, in part, to bigger price level jumps than anticipated and, in part, to structural problems in the financial sector.[4] Indeed, these problems, and the associated capital market failures, may have contributed to the collapse of CMEA trade.

Stabilization policies were necessary to deal with the price surges that occurred in all of these countries, particularly in Bulgaria, Poland, and Romania, where liberalization followed long periods when prices had generally remained fixed and had played virtually no allocative role.[5] Monetary overhang in several of the countries, combined with large budget deficits, further exacerbated inflationary pressures.

In implementing stabilization programs, several countries combined a planned contraction in money and credit in real terms with efforts to restrain real wages, with significant currency depreciations and fiscal adjustment. These policies succeeded to some extent in moderating inflation and reducing public sector deficits. The decline in deficits may appear puzzling given the decline in output, but the explanation lies in the artificial, sharp increase in enterprise profits that followed

---

[2]Sachs (1991) has argued that in Poland, when private sector output is fully taken into account, the overall decline may be less; for an alternative view, see Kolodko (1991). For a discussion of the index number problems that result from rapid price changes and the elimination of shortages, see Osband (1992).

[3]For a discussion of the role played by the collapse of CMEA trade and changes in the terms of trade following a shift to world prices, see Kenen (1991) and Williamson (1991).

[4]The problem of inadequate, or misallocated, credit has been examined in detail in the context of Poland (see Calvo and Coricelli, 1992). The argument is that, in addition to a contractionary effect on demand, credit contraction at the beginning of the stabilization program (including in inter-enterprise credit that followed the withdrawal of the central bank from its role as unconditional "lender of last resort") reduced enterprises' ability to finance their productive activities, thereby lowering aggregate supply. Although there is considerable disagreement on the magnitude of the effect on output in Poland, there is a consensus that an increase in credit now, given the inefficient banking sector, will not necessarily lead to a revival of activity.

[5]This is truer of Bulgaria, Czechoslovakia, and Romania than of Hungary and Poland, where a substantial proportion of prices had not been completely fixed for some time.

Table 1. Eastern Europe: Recent Economic Developments

Country	1987	1988	1989	1990	1991	1992[1]
Bulgaria						
Real GDP (percent change)	5.4	2.6	−0.5	−10.6	−23.0	−3.0
Consumer prices (percent change)[2]	2.7	2.4	6.4	26.3	460.4	49.4
Current account (percent of GDP)[3]	−2.8	−3.6	−5.9	−5.5	−12.1	−18.5
General government balance (cash) (percent of GDP)	−5.1	−5.6	−1.4	−8.5	−3.7	−3.5
International debt[4] (billion U.S. dollars)	6.1	8.2	9.2	10.0	11.8	13.5
Czechoslovakia						
Real GDP (percent change)[5]	2.1	2.3	0.7	−0.4	−15.9	−5.0
Consumer prices (percent change)	0.1	0.2	1.4	10.8	58.7	10.2
Current account (percent of GDP)	0.7	2.1	1.9	−2.9	2.9	2.0
General government balance (percent of GDP)	−0.7	−1.5	−2.4	0.1	−2.0	−4.4
International debt (billion U.S. dollars)	6.7	7.3	7.9	8.2	9.6	9.9
Hungary						
Real GDP (percent change)	4.1	−0.1	−0.2	−4.3	−10.2	−5.0
Consumer prices (percent change)	8.6	14.8	18.9	33.4	32.2	22.0
Current account (percent of GDP)[3]	−3.4	−2.9	−4.9	0.4	0.9	2.7
General government balance (percent of GDP)	−3.5	—	−1.3	0.4	−3.3	−10.6
International debt[3] (billion U.S. dollars)	19.6	19.6	20.4	21.3	21.0	20.8
Poland						
Real GDP (percent change)	2.0	4.1	0.2	−11.6	−7.2	−1.0
Consumer prices (percent change)	25.2	60.2	251.1	585.8	70.3	45.6
Current account (percent of GDP)[3]	−0.6	−0.8	−2.7	1.1	−2.5	−0.2
General government balance (percent of GDP)	−0.8	—	−7.4	3.1	−5.6	−7.2
International debt (billion U.S. dollars)	33.5	39.1	40.8	49.0	48.4	48.6
Romania						
Real GDP (percent change)	0.8	−0.5	−5.8	−7.4	−13.7	−10.0
Consumer prices (percent change)	1.2	2.6	0.9	4.7	161.1	203.0
Current account[3] (percent of GDP)	—	. . .	13.1	−8.0	−6.5	−4.6
General government balance (percent of GDP)	7.0	5.9	8.4	−0.5	−2.6	−1.9
International debt (billion U.S. dollars)	6.1	2.0	0.8	0.9	1.8	3.1

Sources: IMF, recent economic development reports, and staff estimates.
[1] Preliminary estimates.
[2] Average retail prices.
[3] In convertible currencies.
[4] End of year.
[5] Real net material product through 1989.

price liberalization, when enterprises' inventories (including raw materials and intermediate goods) continued to be valued at their historic cost. The resultant increase in profits, illusory though it was, nevertheless had the effect of inflating corporate tax revenues. The current account position of some of these countries improved significantly as well, reflecting a sharp decline in domestic demand and, in Poland in 1990 and Hungary in 1990–91, strong export growth. Although these economies seem to be stabilizing, there has been concern that, together with the decline in output, the volatility in some key economic variables, including domestic prices, real earnings, interest rates, and growth and velocity of money, has exacerbated uncertainty about the structural changes that will be required to complete these countries' transition to market economies. As the discussion below emphasizes, both of these developments may be, in part, related to the misallocation of credit through the existing financial intermediaries.

Role of the Financial Sector

In a market economy, the financial sector mobilizes savings and allocates them among competing ends, facilitates transactions, and prices and allocates risk. It is also instrumental in the pursuit of stabilization policies and in structural transformation.[6] Rapid development and efficient functioning of the financial sector in the transforming economies is therefore crucial. Without active money and credit markets, appropriate monetary policy instruments will be lacking, and, in any case, the transmission mechanisms will be unreliable, making policies less effective.

The issue in the PCPEs has not been simply to liberalize a repressed financial system but rather to reform basic institutions and to design, create, and develop a market-oriented system. They are undertaking this task in an environment where, despite some recent major achievements in price and trade liberalization, several of the basic institutions of a market economy are still lacking. The legal structure relating to property rights and a broadly based private productive sector are in the early stages of development; a market economy ethos is still not fully in place.

The capital stock in all the PCPEs is partially obsolete and generally inefficient. Although, in the past, most of these countries had relatively high saving and investment rates, savings were often channeled toward unproductive and inefficient investments. The financial sector must be able to mobilize savings (both domestic and foreign) and to channel them into domestic investment that is profitable at world market prices if these countries are to attain sustained economic growth.

Financial repression, especially in conjunction with high and unstable inflation, can severely impede growth. It is manifested in a number of ways; for example, savings instruments are underdeveloped, and the real return on savings is negative, leading to low saving rates and to the channeling of savings into unproductive activities. At the same time, asset holders seek protection by holding foreign currency-denominated assets or, if possible, by shifting their assets abroad. Because of the uncertainties generated by inflation, enterprises do not undertake sufficient investment. There is, however, growing evidence to suggest that too rapid financial liberalization under conditions of macroeconomic instability and inadequate bank supervision can lead to high and volatile real interest rates, which can exacerbate financial instability and be detrimental to productive investment (Sundararajan and Baliño, 1991). The evidence emphasizes that the underlying problems—related to a narrow tax base and large budgetary deficits (as well as sharp income inequalities)—that influence the governments' ability to undertake rapid policy adjustments should be tackled at the same time as financial liberalization (Dornbusch and Reynoso, 1989).

There is a consensus that financial liberalization can improve resource allocation; however, there is less agreement as to whether or not it can substantially increase the saving rate (Borensztein and Montiel, 1991). To the extent that financial liberalization in the PCPEs reduces liquidity constraints on households, the precautionary motive for saving might be weakened. In addition, the development of consumer credit markets might increase the indebtedness of the household sector, again leading to a temporary fall in savings. However, the availability of a greater range of savings instruments, with positive real returns, is likely to stimulate overall saving. Furthermore, the increase in uncertainty engendered by the transition, with regard to employment opportunities and the future of social safety nets, may, in fact, lead to greater precautionary saving.

III Development of the Financial Sector

This section describes the prereform financial system in the PCPEs and discusses the main reforms these countries have instituted to date in the banking sector. As a result of the reforms, the central banks have divested themselves of their commercial banking operations and instituted a "two-tier" banking system. However, a large proportion of the newly instituted banks are state-owned; although financial markets—money markets, in particular—are developing, equity markets are in their infancy or are nonexistent.

Prereform Financial System

Before the PCPEs began reforming their economies in the late 1980s, the financial sector was virtually passive. The role of the state largely obviated the need for intermediation, with the financial sector ignoring risk and accommodating the credit demands of the state plan. Under the "monobank system," the financial sector was dominated by the central bank, which, in addition to regulating foreign exchange transactions, acted as banker to the enterprise sector through its credit departments. It was complemented by specialized banks, often fewer than five, which operated in specific sectors of the economy. The central bank set credit policy guidelines, which were approved by the government together with the national economic plan and which determined how the specialized banks allocated credit, and how much they allocated, to the enterprise sector.

In such a system, interest rates had virtually no allocative role, indirect monetary policy instruments were nonexistent, and financial flows were segmented; in particular, the household sector was effectively separated from the enterprise sector. Of the specialized banks, a development bank financed investment projects funded by budgetary transfers; a foreign trade bank specialized in foreign currency and trade financing of enterprises; and a savings bank, acting mainly as banker to the household sector, collected savings deposits at low interest rates and made loans for housing. The state transferred funds from banks with excess deposits (the savings banks) to banks engaged primarily in lending. There was no competition among banks, and money and capital markets were nonexistent.

The bulk of domestic investment, including investment in physical infrastructure and communications, was financed from the budget and enterprise contributions, as well as from internally generated funds in profitable enterprises. Liquidity in these enterprises was controlled through credit ceilings, through forced early repayment of credits, and occasionally through confiscation of profits. Unprofitable enterprises were given access to budgetary support and bank credit, reflecting the "soft budget constraint."[7] They received working capital credit almost automatically to guarantee their wage payments. For the household sector, savings consisted mainly of currency holdings and bank deposits. Except where there were substantial forced savings, the household sector's saving rate was low because of virtually guaranteed lifetime employment, negative real returns on savings, and the availability of heavily subsidized housing loans.

Reforms and the Two-Tier Banking System

Several Eastern European countries undertook to reform their banking sectors even before formally introducing a two-tier banking system. Hungary, for instance, separated central banking and commercial banking operations within the central bank several years before introducing the two-tier system. Savings cooperatives were also authorized to provide banking services similar to those of the national savings bank, and enterprises both in Hungary and Poland were allowed greater freedom to place their time deposits. However, the key features of the traditional system remained in place,

---

[7]This term is used by Kornai (1986) to describe a key feature of enterprise operations in the prereform era. As the discussion in the next section suggests, despite recent reforms, the soft budget constraint persists in many countries.

Table 2. Eastern Europe: Financial Sector Reforms

Country	Two-Tier Banking System	Number and Type of New Banks	Degree of Competition	Capital-Asset Ratio	Share of Bad Loans	Money and Capital Markets	Government Financing	Privatization
Bulgaria	Since March 1990.	Over sixty general and commercial; most localized and too small to be efficient.	Low; major customers of banks also shareholders.	Undercapitalized; minimum requirement to be finalized once banking laws passed.	At the end of 1991, about 40 percent of credit to enterprises deemed unserviceable.	Banks allowed to conduct transactions in commercial paper and securities since June 1990; no stock market.	Bank credit and bonds.	Banks owned by state or enterprises; modest number of small enterprises leased; all large enterprises state-owned.
Czechoslovakia	Since January 1990.	Seven major commercial/ savings banks and nearly thirty small commercial/ specialized banks.	Low, but increasing with the establishment of new banks; segmentation still prevalent.	Some provisioning undertaken, but still low (around 6 percent in late 1992).	Considerable uncertainty, but could be in the range of 15–20 percent.	Money markets being developed; stock market planned for the end of 1992.	Bank credit; bills and bonds since early 1992.	Major banks state-owned. First "wave" of large-scale voucher privatization (1,500 enterprises including banks), to be completed end of 1992. Large share of small enterprises already privatized, and some large-scale joint ventures concluded.
Hungary	Since January 1987.	Thirty commercial banks offering a range of services.	Relatively high, owing in part to the arrival of foreign banks.	After a transitional period, will match Bank for International Settlements (BIS) standards.	Precise estimates lacking but likely to be in the range of 15–20 percent.	Active money market; small stock market established in June 1990 but trading is still thin.	Bank credit, treasury bills, and bonds.	A small share of equity of a number of banks privately held; nearly 400 medium and large nonfinancial enterprises privatized.

| Poland | Since January 1989. | Nine major banks; over fifty small ones (accounting for over 5 percent of total credit). | Owing to regional concentration, competition limited, but arrival of foreign banks likely to provide a spur. | Attempts will be made to match BIS standards by 1993, but it could affect credit significantly. | At end-1991, around 30 percent. Seven of the nine major banks had bad loans ranging from 25 percent to 60 percent of their portfolio. | Money market established in 1990; stock market established in April 1991. | Bank credit, treasury bills, and, recently, treasury bonds with maturities of one and three years. | Major bank state-owned; many small banks privately owned. All retail and wholesale trade privatized, but only a small number of large industrial enterprises privatized. |
| Romania | Since December 1990. | Fewer than ten; specialized/ general. | Relatively low. | Recently introduced guidelines below BIS standards. | In 1990, a large proportion of bad loans written off; but the problem has re-emerged. | Money markets being planned. | Bank credit; bond financing planned. | A few small private banks; privatization of enterprises to begin in earnest in 1992. |

Source: IMF staff.

with segmentation of the household and enterprise sectors, central credit allocation, and administered interest rates.

Hungary established a two-tier banking system in 1987, Poland in 1989, and Bulgaria, Czechoslovakia, and Romania in 1990, prompting the central banks to divest themselves of their commercial banking operations (Table 2). This, in turn, led to a separation of financial intermediation from monetary control functions, with the central banks assuming the traditional function of regulating overall credit and interest rates. The financial intermediation operations were taken over by the newly instituted commercial banks—in the main, the old specialized banks—which were henceforth to be operated according to market criteria. The regulatory environment was liberalized to permit freedom in lending and to allow these banks to provide a wide range of services. They continue to be state-owned, and a significant proportion of their portfolios consists of deposits and loans made in the prereform period. Many of the loans include credits to essentially insolvent enterprises as well as loans at highly concessional rates. At the same time, new, often privately owned, commercial banks were established. They were unable, however, to compete for deposits and loans owing to the dominance of the old specialized banks.

The new banking system is in its infancy, and, despite a mushrooming of new private banks in nearly all countries, the overwhelming proportion of financial intermediation is undertaken by the state-owned commercial banks. As Table 2 illustrates, there is marked diversity in the structure of the financial sectors across the PCPEs, for instance, in the number of commercial banks, in their modes of operation, and in the type of competition among them. However, there are a number of key common features, including the poor quality of banks' loan portfolios, their continuing specialization, and, despite the increasing number of banks, the limited competition among them. Furthermore, the financial markets are currently dominated by the banking sector: short-term money markets are in the early stages of development, and medium- and long-term capital markets either lack depth or are nonexistent.

Some progress has been made in changing instruments of monetary control from the detailed credit allocation process to various direct and indirect controls, such as central bank refinancing quotas, bank-specific credit ceilings, reserve requirements, and special deposits with the central banks (see Sundararajan, 1990). For example, Czechoslovakia, Hungary, and Poland have introduced some market-based instruments, such as treasury or central bank bill auctions. Whereas interest rates have been largely liberalized in Bulgaria and Hungary, different degrees of control remain in Czechoslovakia, Poland, and Romania. At the same time, direct ceilings on the volume of credit remain in several countries; the refinance rate—the rate at which funds can be obtained from central banks—has become the key interest rate influencing or guiding deposit and lending rates in several countries. As part of the stabilization measures, real interest rates have been substantially increased, often to high positive levels. But flexible management of interest rates has proved difficult because of the structural problems relating to the banking sector and because of the difficulty of extending market-based instruments of monetary control, which require adequate flows of information supported by speedy and reliable accounting procedures and settlement arrangements.

A key aspect of the reforms is to enable the banking sector to play a key role in providing savings instruments, credit, and a payments mechanism. It is too early, however, to distinguish the impact of increased financial intermediation and the availability of financial instruments from that of broader macroeconomic developments, such as price and trade liberalization. For instance, sharp increases in the inflation rate in Poland in 1990 and in other countries in 1991 led to a significant drawdown in household financial assets, reflecting high negative real returns and a greater availability of consumer goods.

Data in Table 3 and Chart 1 show that, from 1990 to 1991, credit declined relative to GDP in nearly all of the PCPEs. In particular, credit outstanding to the enterprise sector appears to have declined steeply in some of them. Although stabilization programs in several PCPEs projected declines in real credit to control inflation, actual declines were sometimes greater, owing, in part, to higher-than-expected inflation. But, the explanation probably also lies partly in structural factors, which adversely affected the banks' ability and willingness to provide credit (Section IV).[8]

---

[8]It is also useful to compare the experience of PCPEs with recent successful stabilization programs in other developing countries. There is clear evidence that real credit increased fairly soon after an initial decline in these countries (see Bruno and Meridor (1991) for the case of Israel, and Ortiz (1991) for Mexico).

Table 3. Eastern Europe: Domestic Credit[1]
(In percent of GDP)

A. Total Domestic Credit

Country	1987	1988	1989	1990	1991
Bulgaria	111.2	120.9	130.5	133.6	84.2
Czechoslovakia	67.3	68.3	72.7	74.7	72.1
Hungary	97.2	92.2	83.4	78.6	77.6
Poland	44.4	33.8	26.1	12.5	23.8
Romania	56.5	56.6	62.0	66.9	39.2

B. Credit to Enterprise and Household Sectors

Country	1987	1988	1989	1990	1991
Bulgaria	107.7	112.9	118.5	112.8	60.6
Czechoslovakia	80.3	79.6	76.5	71.0	66.0
Hungary	64.9	61.7	49.3	42.7	42.0
Poland	43.8	32.1	22.6	12.7	18.8
Romania	87.1	94.5	101.7	88.4	35.8

C. Credit to Nonfinancial Public Enterprises

Country	1987	1988	1989	1990	1991
Bulgaria	97.1	101.5	106.2	99.2	54.7
Czechoslovakia	74.5	73.5	70.3	65.1	62.0
Hungary	30.9	27.4	24.8	25.7	28.1
Poland	39.9	29.1	21.0	11.1	15.2
Romania	89.2	94.5	101.7	88.5	40.9

Source: IMF staff estimates.
[1] Average of beginning and end of period.

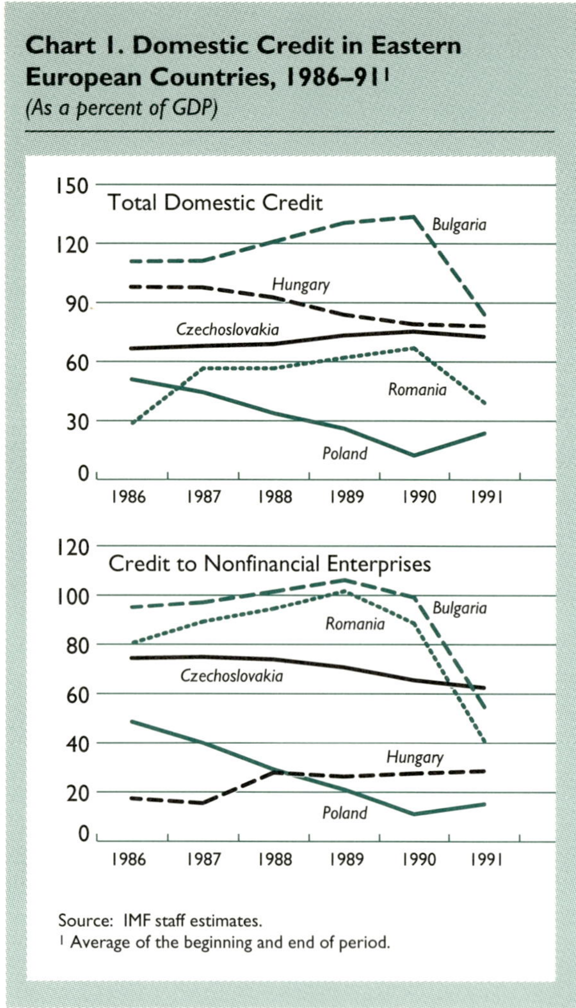

Chart 1. Domestic Credit in Eastern European Countries, 1986–91[1]
(As a percent of GDP)
Total Domestic Credit
Bulgaria
Hungary
Czechoslovakia
Romania
Poland
150
120
90
60
30
0
1986 1987 1988 1989 1990 1991
Credit to Nonfinancial Enterprises
Bulgaria
Romania
Czechoslovakia
Hungary
Poland
120
100
80
60
40
20
0
1986 1987 1988 1989 1990 1991
Source: IMF staff estimates.
[1] Average of the beginning and end of period.

One of the key problems facing the newly constituted commercial banks is the poor quality of loan portfolios. This section discusses the problem and suggests several approaches for dealing with it. However, even if the problem of the loan portfolios could be resolved quickly, the banking sector would still not be efficient, and the portfolio problem would recur unless the enterprise sector is also restructured. This section also highlights the lack of competition in the banking sector, notes its implication for banks' efficiency and the cost of capital, and outlines steps to encourage it.

Quality of Loan Portfolios

The unsatisfactory quality of the loan portfolios of the newly created commercial banks derived from the transition to the market system. Under the system of central planning, the financial flows of the household and enterprise sectors were separate. Thus, when commercial banks were created, their asset portfolios consisted overwhelmingly of enterprise loans. Given the administrative allocation of financial resources and soft budget constraints, enterprises had been allowed to service outstanding loans through additional borrowing. The collapse of CMEA trade, declines in output, and significant changes in relative prices have adversely affected the profitability of enterprises and compounded the difficulties for banks' balance sheets. The banks are generally undercapitalized and, if their loans were to be revalued realistically, many of them would be insolvent.

Although the precise magnitude of the portfolio problem is not known, there is a general consensus that it is significant, with large differences across countries. At the end of 1991, in Poland, 20–30 percent of banks' assets were estimated to be substandard. Recent audits of seven of its nine state-owned commercial banks suggest that between 25 percent and 60 percent of their loan portfolios are substandard, whereas, according to the banks, substandard loans amount to about 16 percent of total credit to nongovernment. Inflation, which has been higher in Poland than in the other Eastern European countries, initially reduced the real value of enterprises' existing debt, but the old loans were generally rolled over at a higher interest rate, thus eroding the benefit of high inflation for the debtors. New loans continued to be provided to enterprises that were unable to service existing loans. Furthermore, the continued changes in relative prices and the worsening of economic conditions have probably caused the quality of the portfolios to deteriorate. Recent estimates, for instance, indicate that nearly 2,700 state-owned enterprises, accounting for about one-third of the industrial output in Poland, are deemed to have lost creditworthiness.

In Bulgaria, nonperforming loans are reported to exceed 40 percent of the banks' loan portfolios, and even this figure is regarded as low. The problem can be assessed only after market-clearing prices have been fully established and financial discipline is imposed on enterprises; indeed, the problem may have been aggravated by the increase in real interest rates over the last year or so. Similarly, in Czechoslovakia and Hungary, 15–20 percent of loans are regarded as unserviceable. In comparison, if in an industrial country unserviceable loans amount to between 2 percent and 4 percent of a bank's asset portfolio, its situation is generally regarded as potentially serious.

The balance sheet difficulties of banks are related to the problem of inter-enterprise claims. These claims, which derive largely from arrears to suppliers, account for a sizable proportion of enterprises' debt. In Poland, for instance, at the end of 1990, these claims amounted to 155 percent of banking system credit to the socialized sector (Lane, 1992). The increase in claims has been a response by enterprises to circumvent the strict credit ceilings. Although some of the debts can be netted out within the enterprise sector, a large proportion corresponds to an increase in the enterprises' net debt to banks; if one enterprise does not repay another, the latter may not be able to repay the interest on its existing loans. Thus, although banks do not increase credit, interest arrears arise, and the number of nonperforming loans—but not the number of new loans—rises. A clampdown on inter-enterprise credit without any other accompanying measure could exacerbate the banks' problem and would quickly cause a significant number of enterprises to become insolvent, which could lead to open insolvency in the banking sector. Thus, policies to deal with banks' balance sheets cannot be pursued in isolation from policies dealing with enterprises' financial situation.

The poor quality of loan portfolios is likely to have a number of consequences: first, the willingness of banks to recognize loans as nonperforming will be limited, thereby encouraging continued lending to weak enterprises. This inhibits the enforcement of financial discipline on enterprises, which, whether they are restructuring or expanding their operations, need discipline because it is not being enforced by shareholders, capital markets, or other agents. Second, because of credit ceilings and high interest rates, profitable enterprises could face a credit crunch, and their investment and output activities may be adversely affected. Because the prospective profitability of enterprises is highly uncertain, banks have tended to make loans largely to keep unprofitable enterprises afloat, which provides a semblance of solvency, rather than allowing others, which are potentially profitable at world prices, to expand operations. Third, privatization of the banks is delayed because it is difficult to attract private, especially external, investors who are interested either in purchasing the banks outright or in equity participation.

There are three possible approaches for dealing with poor loan portfolios. First, nonperforming loans on banks' books could be replaced with interest-bearing government debt. Although it is unlikely that all such loans can be identified, a high proportion of them could be. This approach would have the merit of conserving banks' total asset base while helping to increase their soundness. Since most banks and large enterprises are still state-owned, this step may appear to represent essentially a transfer within the state sector. Although the recorded level of public debt would increase, there would be no significant inflationary effect. However, because government revenues are already inadequate, while the needs for public sector investment, especially in infrastructure and communications, will be substantial, this approach may overstretch the government's revenue capacity. This, in turn, may have adverse implications for the credibility of the stabilization programs these countries are currently pursuing.

If governments are to help recapitalization take place by issuing debt to the banks, a number of important questions concerning the characteristics of the debt must be answered. For instance, should it be short term or long term, and at fixed or floating interest rates? These questions have implications not only for the banking sector—if maturity mismatches occur between the asset and liability sides of banks' balance sheets—but also for monetary and fiscal policy.

A second approach would involve some type of monetary reform whereby both the nominal assets and the liabilities of banks *vis-à-vis the enterprises* are written off. That is, the assets of the enterprise sector are set off against the banking sector's liabilities. The elimination of enterprises' deposits could be justified on the same basis as was the removal of bad loans from the banks' portfolios. Both measures reflect past developments that should not be allowed to hamper the future operations of either banks or enterprises. In this sense, the second approach may be appropriate only if implemented at the outset of structural reforms. If undertaken one or two years after reforms are initiated, it would affect the deposits of newly profitable firms and hamper the hoped-for restructuring. Nevertheless, the approach imposes no additional burden on public finances, and the credibility of further public sector debt finance would not be threatened.[9] Since household deposits need not be affected, the approach may be more acceptable politically.

A third approach would be to have banks make provision for the nonperforming loans out of their own current profits. In several countries, measured bank profits have appeared to be high although there is considerable uncertainty about their actual value owing to the rollover of unserviceable loans. Furthermore, the scale of the problem implies that such loan-loss provisions from the banks' own resources are likely to be inadequate and, therefore, will ultimately require direct budgetary support. (Setting aside these provisions would also mean that tax revenues from banks' profits would be reduced.) If, over time, the countries were to adopt deposit insurance schemes, these could provide an additional mechanism for dealing with

---

[9]See Dornbusch and Wolf (1990) for a discussion of the role that such "monetary reform" played in European countries in the aftermath of World War II. They argue that, compared with all other methods, a write-down of financial assets and liabilities is the one most likely to strengthen confidence in the ability and willingness of a government to meet its commitments. They conclude that governments that have eliminated a debt overhang will look better than governments that appear willing to honor their liabilities but are patently unable to do so.

the weak portfolios. This mechanism would be more useful, however, for establishing confidence in the system than for dealing with the above problem. In any case, unless insurance premiums were to become extremely high, recourse to budgetary funds might eventually become necessary again.

Thus, the choice is essentially between the first two approaches—cleaning banks' balance sheets and monetary reform. While the two approaches differ markedly in their implications for public sector finances, they share two related problems. The first is that of moral hazard: banks might appear to be bailed out, which could be regarded as a bad precedent in the transition to a market economy. Second, unless the environment in which enterprises operate changes significantly, with a commitment to the hard budget constraint and the institution of proper incentives, a onetime cleaning of banks' loan portfolios would be, at best, a temporary measure.

Several of the PCPEs have taken the first steps toward reform. Romania, for instance, used large budgetary surpluses to write off a substantial part of nonperforming loans; however, there are already signs that the problem is re-emerging. Czechoslovakia transferred Kcs 110 billion in credits (about one-sixth of all banking loans) to a consolidation bank, but it was unclear how these loans were to be dealt with; more recently, the National Property Funds have issued Kcs 50 billion in bonds to be used for the replacement of bad loans and the capitalization of banks. Hungary has completed an audit of the banks and is likely to use a combination of the first and third approaches. In Bulgaria, the choice of approach is to be addressed as part of a structural adjustment loan by the World Bank.

Finally, it is worth noting how the problem was addressed in the former German Democratic Republic. Although a special case, given the availability of significant external financing and expertise, and because it immediately adopted the price structure of an advanced market economy, it provides an example of a major recent banking reform. Under its approach—a form of budgetary support—the sole commercial bank, Kreditbank, entered into joint ventures with two large west German commercial banks. The two west German banks were able to use branch offices of Kreditbank, while the entire portfolio of old loans to east German enterprises remained with Kreditbank, which was reduced to a shell holding company. The new banks have no direct interest in pressing for the repayment of loans, and the enterprises have a clear incentive to default. In fact, in the face of

mounting debt-servicing problems, reflecting difficulties faced by the enterprises, a year-long moratorium was declared on the servicing of debt. In the meantime, the Kreditbank's liabilities are being serviced by grants from the west German Government (Brainard, 1991).

Enterprise Restructuring and Credit Allocation

An additional problem in the PCPEs is the banks' lack of experience in assessing the creditworthiness of enterprises. Most bank employees have been trained in the traditional monobank system, under which the concepts of profitability and risk were either irrelevant or, at best, secondary. It will take them time to become versed in market-oriented credit allocation criteria.

Another, more important, reason for the inefficient intermediation of banks is the lack of proper enterprise accounts, compounded by the rapidly changing situation, including significant changes in relative prices that make it difficult to determine the potential profitability of enterprises and investment projects. The difficulty is exacerbated by the fact that the existing balance sheets of enterprises, representing their past liabilities, do not necessarily reflect their underlying profitability. In this context, a recent study concluded that distortions of domestic prices had been large enough to vitiate the use of profitability or value added as a measure of industries' solvency. According to the estimates, some 20–25 percent of industries in the PCPEs had negative value added when measured at world prices. These conclusions are, however, based, in some cases, on prices prevailing before market-oriented reforms were initiated (Hughes and Hare, 1991).

These findings support the contention that cleaning banks' books must be accompanied by a reorganization of the enterprises that includes cleaning their balance sheets. This measure would prevent them from being weighed down by their inherited liabilities and allow banks to judge their prospective operating potential and creditworthiness. The incentive structure must also be changed, so that enterprises respond to market signals and base operating decisions primarily on profitability. In this regard, enforcing the hard budget constraint is important. Despite the sharp declines in output in all PCPEs, there have been virtually no enterprise bankruptcies because, with few exceptions, soft budget constraints continue, and governments are therefore unable to credibly threaten not to bail out unprofitable firms. (The main exception is

Hungary, where bankruptcy proceedings have been initiated against many firms.)

In such a situation, privatization of enterprises becomes relevant. Large-scale privatizations are not currently feasible in all countries because, given the uncertain prospects of most enterprises and the dearth of private investors, it may be difficult to sell them. But if enterprises and banks continue to be state-owned, the banks would be pressured to bail out enterprises that experience serious financial difficulties. Recent reforms do not appear to have changed this situation markedly. It is therefore essential to introduce private ownership to put the appropriate constraints, and the incentive structure, in place.

Competition in the Banking Sector

A third area of concern, which is related to portfolio quality, is the small number of commercial banks and the lack of competition among them.[10] The lack of effective competition is due partly to the legacy of the old system and partly to continuing entry barriers, which are reflected in the absence of an adequate and transparent regulatory framework. Despite many joint ventures, or fully foreign-owned banks, as in Hungary and Poland, the continuing uncertainty about the macroeconomic environment and the pace of reforms is eroding these banks' incentive to expand their operations and stifling further competition from abroad.

A number of implications are associated with the lack of competition. First, the banks have little incentive to improve the efficiency of their operations or to increase the range of services they offer. (Against this, it should be noted that the minimum efficient size of the banks may be quite large, given economies of scale and the underdeveloped nature of the markets.)[11]

Second, where the government has not set deposit and loan rates, banks have had excessive spreads, reflecting the high interest rates charged to borrowers. Although some of the high spreads may represent default risk premiums on loans made to the enterprise sector, they may also simply reflect monopolistic power. Even if banks could set aside excessive profits as provision against bad debts, the larger spreads are difficult to justify. High loan rates increase the cost of capital and discourage capital investment, and, in any case, there is no certainty that banks will continue to use the excess profits for provisioning. Third, the lack of competition can make the conduct of monetary policy inefficient. For example, owing to the lack of depth in the financial markets and the absence of appropriate instruments, the central bank has to rely on direct controls in deciding on the amount and allocation of credit.

To stimulate competition, the regulatory and legal framework must be developed and made more transparent. In particular, the regulatory and legal situation must be clarified, and the barriers to entry need to be reduced. Transparent rules for supervising and monitoring banks and clear guidelines on the role of the central bank could also spur domestic competition. These measures alone, however, may not be enough to increase entry and competition. Also required are skilled personnel and financial resources, both of which foreign banks could provide.

In summary, cleaning banks' balance sheets would be only a first step toward reorganizing the banking sector along market lines. Equally important is the reform of enterprises, which will need to be restructured radically or privatized before banks can undertake market-oriented decisions and begin to channel credit to the most productive sectors.

---

[10]Here again, there are significant differences across countries. In Bulgaria, for instance, the transformation in 1989 of the former Bulgarian National Bank into independent banks has resulted in the creation of a large number of small banks. But because these banks do not have a branch network, competition is still weak. In Czechoslovakia, there are only a handful of commercial banks (essentially the old specialized banks) and a number of new private banks, with a limited number of branches. Poland has nine large commercial banks and a large number of small banks, but the competition among them has been very limited.

[11]There is considerable evidence from both industrial and developing countries that suggests significant economies of scale in financial intermediation. Moreover, the scarcity of trained personnel argues for a limited number of financial institutions. At the same time, excessive concentration leads to higher loan rates, a reduction in service, and higher bank profits, giving rise to a nonlinear concentration-profit relationship. (See, for instance, Gilbert, 1984.)

V Privatization and Capital Markets

Although the PCPEs have begun to reform their banking sectors, serious problems remain. At the same time, long-term capital markets, including equity and bond markets, remain underdeveloped. It is useful to examine the role that capital markets, especially equity markets, can play in restructuring the enterprise sector, for example, by mobilizing and channeling long-term capital to enterprises and providing a mechanism for monitoring and evaluating their operations. While there is a consensus that capital markets are crucial in the long run, there is less agreement on the pace at which the markets can be developed and the form they should take.

It has been argued, for instance, that because of the time and resources that may be required to develop these markets, the PCPEs would be better off focusing on the development of commercial banks (Volcker, 1990; Brainard, 1991). Once the commercial banks are put on a sound footing, they could be the main channel for providing finance to a restructured enterprise sector. Where restructuring creates a need for particularly long-term finance, floating rate instruments can be used judiciously to avoid excessive risks to the banking sector. In addition, other aspects of financial sector reform, including development of the payments and auditing systems, and banking supervision and regulation, should be given priority. Furthermore, even if capital markets start functioning on a basic level fairly soon, their lack of depth and breadth could make them susceptible to high volatility.

Notwithstanding the validity of the above arguments, the role that banks can play is seriously limited. This raises a number of questions concerning the extent to which capital markets in the uncertain and volatile market environment of the PCPEs can complement the emerging commercial banking system, in particular, by providing medium- and long-term risk capital. These markets currently provide relatively little new finance to the business sector in industrial countries; however, they are important in the developing countries. Even in the industrial countries, there is evidence that, at a developmental phase similar to the one through which the PCPEs are now passing, equity markets played an important role. (See Singh and Hamid, 1992; Appendix.)

Equity Markets

The creation and development of equity markets are likely to be subject to a number of constraints and many risks. But, to enjoy the potential benefits of the markets, it will be necessary to take some of these risks. The benefits include risk sharing in the provision of long-term finance, imposition of a degree of control over enterprises, and a focus for foreign portfolio investments.

The most important benefit PCPEs will derive from the development of equity markets is the provision of risk capital and the diversification of risks. Given the prevalent climate of instability, both enterprises and banks will be less inclined to undertake investments that have uncertain payoffs, even if banks' balance sheets and efficiency improve considerably. As a result, potentially profitable enterprises may simply not be able to get adequate funds because banks, tending to prefer well-established, safe borrowers, may not allocate capital efficiently. Equity markets can finance the risky yet productive borrowers that bankers avoid (see, for instance, Diamond, 1991). This problem can be alleviated considerably through the creation of markets that allow enterprises to issue equity to the general public. A wide ownership of firms' common shares allows the risk associated with any new project to be spread across many stockholders, who, in turn, can diversify across different enterprises. This diversification can reduce, or eliminate, the unsystematic risk of investment and, hence, increase the availability of capital as well as lower the risk premium component in its cost. In developing countries, furthermore, the announcement of seasoned stock offerings is often considered a positive signal because investors view them as a sign of profitable investment opportunities for the firm (Kim, 1990). (An excessive dispersion of equity shares can, however, have adverse consequences for supervision and control of enterprises.)

Equity markets can also provide a mechanism for owners to exercise supervisory functions. The continuous valuation of share prices and the implied possibility of mergers and takeovers can impose discipline on the investment behavior of firms. Similarly, by effecting changes in management—a scarce resource in the PCPEs—equity markets can enhance the efficiency with which management resources are used.

Finally, capital markets provide institutional investors in developed countries, such as mutual funds, pension funds, and insurance companies, with instruments to diversify their assets geographically, thus increasing the potential for significant inflows of portfolio investment. Even a small increase in institutional investors' desired stock of assets in the PCPEs could produce a dramatic increase in the flows of foreign capital. The volume of these flows will, of course, depend on the development of the markets, the prospective returns, the tax and regulatory environment, and the availability of accounting and financial information on the restructured enterprises.

The above benefits suggest that the development of capital markets merits some attention in the context of financial sector reforms in the PCPEs. The main issue is the speed with which the markets can be developed in an environment where the time and the human resources that can be devoted to financial reforms in general are limited. Initially, development of equity markets can be an integral part of the privatization process. Such a process is generally regarded as necessary both for efficiency reasons and for completing the transition to a market economy (Borensztein and Kumar, 1991).

The privatization of a very large number of enterprises is not easy, as evidenced by recent delays. One reason for the delays is that, in the current environment, it has been difficult to calculate accurately the net worth of state enterprises. Moreover, because enterprises' balance sheets and operations have not been restructured, it has not been easy to find potential buyers. The problems of valuation and restructuring could be handled by the creation of holding companies or mutual funds to monitor and supervise the performance of enterprises during privatization. Initially, shares in these holding companies or mutual funds could be sold, or given, to the public, and these companies or funds would, in turn, hold equity in the enterprises. During a fixed period of perhaps one or two years, they would be obliged to restructure the enterprises and sell off their equity stake to the public. Enterprises would have an incentive to provide maximum information to such companies in the expectation of obtaining their "seal of approval" with respect to the accuracy and completeness of their financial information. Such approval could be regarded as crucial to enterprises' attempts to issue new equity subsequently and to maintain, or increase, their market value.

As enterprises are privatized, the equity in the holding companies becomes equity in the enterprises and would be freely tradable on the stock exchanges. Once this happens, enterprises can float new equity shares and begin to attract new capital. This process would be facilitated by the development within the PCPEs of market-oriented non-bank financial institutions, such as pension funds, unit trusts, and insurance companies.[12] Further development of the markets and the ability of enterprises to attract fresh capital would depend critically on the confidence that potential investors have in the markets. Confidence would grow if strict codes to outlaw insider trading and other related practices were instituted.

To provide a perspective for the PCPEs, it should be noted that, in many developing countries, equity markets have grown extremely fast in recent years, and their capitalization exceeds that of several industrial countries. In Korea, for instance, the market has grown almost 40-fold in the past ten years, with market capitalization increasing from 6 percent of GNP in 1980 to over 80 percent by the end of 1990. In India, market capitalization has increased to 9 percent of GDP from 4 percent over the last four years. In terms of overall corporate financing needs, the capital market in these two countries accounted for about 15 percent of gross asset formation during 1980–87 (IFC, 1991).

As exemplified by the experiences of developing countries, the development of equity markets can be enhanced, in particular, by interest rate and taxation policies as well as by more market-specific, regulatory, and institutional features that influence companies' optimal financing mix and investors' asset portfolio composition. Both the demand for and the supply of equities are important. Concerning demand, the return on equities relative to other financial assets is critical. Regarding supply, in some developing countries, the pretax cost of debt has been kept artificially low, with tax deductibility of interest expense at the corporate level further accentuating this effect. This suggests one important reason why firms in some developing countries

---

[12]On the complementarity between equity markets and non-bank financial institutions, see, for instance, Fischer and Merton (1984), and Dailami and Atkin (1990).

have relied on debt and are often more leveraged than are firms in industrial countries (Singh and Hamid, 1992).

Using equity markets involves a number of costs, including the cost inherent in the separation of management and ownership, the efficiency with which project risks are diversified and priced, and, possibly, excessive volatility. The role of markets in takeover activities and their impact on the competitiveness and efficiency of companies have also been scrutinized. It is suggested, for instance, that the takeover threat, or actual takeovers, may weaken companies' competitiveness by inducing a bias toward short-term profits and financial returns. In this context, the performance of U.K. and U.S. companies is contrasted with the bank-based financial systems in Germany and Japan but without yielding convincing results (see Singh and Hamid, 1992). Evidence on this issue is even less systematic for developing countries, but what little evidence there is does not suggest that the takeover mechanism significantly affects firms' operating horizons.

Finally, equity markets in developing countries have been regarded as excessively volatile, and there is concern that such volatility in the PCPEs could be damaging not only to the confidence of the potential investors but also to the financial reforms as a whole. The volatility derives from overly regulated financial sectors, high market concentration, the thinness of trading, and inadequate dissemination of information (Darrat and Mukherjee, 1986).[13] Companies appear to divulge less information with a greater time lag in developing countries than in industrial countries, owing largely to the efforts of the holders of large chunks of equity—frequently individual families—to safeguard their position. In the PCPEs, if equity markets evolve during privatization, then high market concentration is unlikely. However, markets could still be volatile owing to thinness of trading. If the PCPEs adopt the policy measures noted, volatility will be reduced and its adverse effects limited.

Banks and the Privatization Process

Banks have an important role in the privatization process and in the development of the capital markets. They can be involved in industry purely as financial intermediaries or they can directly influence the operations of enterprises. In its role of

creditor, a bank provides loans to an enterprise on commercial terms; that is, it assesses the enterprise's current financial position, its prospective situation, and the profitability and riskiness of its specific investment projects. For a bank to be able to do this, first, reliable and objective accounting and other financial information about the enterprise's operations must be available; second, the bank must be readily able to obtain this information from the enterprise; and, third, the bank must have the techniques and technology to process this information and to judge the enterprise's creditworthiness accurately. The PCPEs are currently weak in all three areas and are likely to be so for some time. This situation is likely to affect adversely both the willingness and the ability of banks to provide adequate funding to newly privatized enterprises, with possible severe consequences for investment and growth. Moreover, if the banks are somehow induced to extend excessively risky loans, the stability of the newly emerging financial system could be further jeopardized.

A number of observers have suggested that rather than weakening prudential supervision or regulation by forcing banks to lend, it may be more appropriate for the banks to become directly involved in restructuring (Blanchard and others, 1991). Given the need for rapid privatization, share ownership by banks could be the best way of privatizing the industrial enterprises for the following reasons: (1) banks are likely to be the only existing financial intermediaries that can absorb large amounts of equity; (2) banks could be among the few existing institutions that can provide corporate governance; (3) a close relationship between industrial enterprises and the banks is especially important when other capital markets are weak or underdeveloped; and (4) more than half the equity in industrial firms is held by financial institutions in most advanced market economies.

However, given the constraints on banks in the PCPEs, it is far from obvious that they will be able to oversee management decisions in a constructive way, a role that, in any case, carries significant risks. Comparison with industrial countries, where macroeconomic conditions are relatively stable and risks of insolvency are limited, may not be appropriate. Unlike the industrial countries, the PCPEs are likely to experience considerable instability during transition, which could seriously compromise the banks' financial position. Furthermore, restructuring and reorganizing enterprises would require that many of them close down. If banks were involved as both owners and creditors, there could be a serious conflict of interest. In addition, banks' income would depend on dividends from the enterprises

---

[13]See Appendix Table 3 for some data on equity market concentration in a sample of developing countries.

as well as on interest charges on loans made to them; the former source could be highly volatile and might lead to excessive volatility in the banks' own income streams.[14]

[14]In this context, the role of banks in the privatization of enterprises in Chile is particularly instructive. In the first phase of privatization during the late 1970s, banks were required to play a major role as owners. When economic conditions deteriorated in the early 1980s, a large number of enterprises became insolvent, making the banks insolvent along with them, leading to a full-scale financial crisis (see Luders, 1991).

In conclusion, the development of equity markets in all PCPEs could complement the development of a market-oriented banking sector. Equity markets would yield substantial benefits by mobilizing and channeling risk capital while also reducing its cost. Privatization could play a key role in the initial development of these markets, but further development would depend on the establishment of an appropriate regulatory framework, with mechanisms to monitor enterprises. The role of banks in the privatization process should, however, be treated with caution.

VI Financial Sector Reforms and Stabilization Policies

This section notes the close linkages between financial sector reform and the conduct of monetary policy, including the recent introduction of indirect instruments of monetary management, and the implications of reforms for the quantitative formulation of monetary targets. It assesses the contribution that financial sector reform can make to the conduct of fiscal policy, in particular, to the financing of budget deficits. The discussion also suggests that the maintenance of current account convertibility requires prompt reform in the financial sector to encourage supply response.

Monetary Policy

There are close linkages between financial sector reform, monetary policy framework, and stabilization and other structural reform policies.[15] Wide-ranging structural changes in the financial sector are a prerequisite of effective and efficient monetary policy, without which progress toward macroeconomic and financial stability would be difficult to achieve. Several countries are replacing the administrative system of monetary control with a system of indirect monetary control, leading to greater efficiency in transmitting changes in government policies to the real economy. In place of bank-specific credit ceilings and selective credit allocations, these countries are emphasizing market forces in credit allocation and introducing discount rates, reserve requirements, and open market operations. Although they have made considerable progress, as seen, for example, in the declining share of automatic central bank refinancing, the use of these market-oriented instruments is still in its early stages (Table 4).

Three aspects of the relationship between financial sector reforms and recent monetary policy are worth noting. First, successful interest rate liberalization—that is, the successful management of interest rates through indirect instruments—requires a relatively stable macroeconomic environment, adequate competition and reasonable financial strength in the banking sector, an active and well-functioning money market, and policy instruments that can influence banks' marginal cost of funds (Leite and Sundararajan, 1990). Difficulties in each of these areas have led several countries to continue to guide banks in setting interest rates on loans and deposits (or more often in limiting bank spreads). (However, the degree of intervention varies considerably across countries; in Bulgaria and Hungary, for instance, it is limited.) The deposit and loan rates have thus not been a function of the strength of loan demand, the supply of deposits, or the creditworthiness of the potential borrowers. In moving toward full interest rate flexibility and more efficient credit allocation, the PCPEs should institute policies to deal with problem loans and parallel reforms of prudential regulations and supervision systems.

Second, the quantitative formulation of monetary policy typically assumes the existence of a relatively stable money demand function. But financial reforms can lead to significant shifts, and hence instability, in the demand for money (Chart 2).[16] Similarly, money supply is no longer simply a function of reserve money since the household and enterprise sectors, as well as the banks, can, to some extent, choose their asset-liability portfolios according to market rates of return and relative risks. Therefore, the money multiplier will respond to changes in income, wealth, and interest rates. The quantitative changes in the structural relationship between the demand for and the supply of money that may be expected to result from the reform process thus need to be taken into account in monetary policy.

---

[15]The subsequent discussion is based on Sundararajan (1990) and Khan and Sundararajan (1991).

[16]In many developing countries undertaking financial sector reforms, the ratios of money and credit to GDP have risen, while the ratio of currency to deposits has declined. Chart 2 illustrates the volatility in the PCPEs, showing marked changes in monetary velocity in several of the countries.

Table 4. Eastern Europe: Monetary Policy

Country	Determination of Interest Rates	Open Market Operations	Reserve Requirements	Credit Ceilings and Effectiveness	Preferential Credit
Bulgaria	Market determined; central bank provides recommendations for term structure. Banks have significant spreads.	Initiated in 1990. In December 1990, one-year treasury bonds were issued to finance part of the budget deficit. In 1991, short-term treasury bills at market-related interest rates were also issued.	Minimum of 7 percent, not used as an active policy instrument.	Bank-by-bank credit ceilings in place since 1990; effective for controlling credit.	Mainly consists of old household loans. No new credit being offered (1991).
Czechoslovakia	Flexible.	Central bank refinance credit increasingly channeled through auctions. Treasury bills issued in 1992; interbank market limited.	Introduced in October 1990, but not used as an active policy instrument.	Credit ceilings by bank used to ration credit. Recently, ceilings on banks removed (for small banks in April 1992 and large banks in October 1992).	Mainly old household loans.
Hungary	Deposit and lending rates freed for the enterprise sector since 1987; deposit rate ceilings for households from 1988 to end-1991.	Began in 1988; became active in 1990–91; both treasury bills and bonds being issued. Active interbank money market.	Initially set mainly for prudential purposes; changed in 1990 to ensure uniformity among financial institutions and to tighten liquidity.	Currently not used as a policy instrument.	Reduced use of preferential credit (primarily used as instrument of credit policy).
Poland	Banks are permitted to set interest rates, but the Central Bank informally influences some spreads.	In 1990, steps were taken to develop a money market. In March, the National Bank of Poland (NBP) initiated auctions in which banks could bid for special deposits. In July, it began issuing bills that could be held either by banks or by nonbank enterprises or individuals. Weekly auctions in NBP and treasury bills. NBP bills withdrawn in 1992.	Reserve requirements were used as one way of absorbing excess liquidity (1990). Initially, a split reserve requirement, later, a unified requirement, was instituted. Then, as reserve requirements were raised to higher levels, a split reserve requirement was re-established, with a lower rate for time deposits.	NBP tried to use moral suasion to restrain credit expansion in the first half of 1990. Bank-by-bank credit ceilings used since 1990.	Underwent significant change in 1990. Agricultural sector was beneficiary. Most important innovation was open-ended credit for procurement of agriculture products (summer 1990). Also preferential credit to housing and central investment projects.
Romania	Generally market determined since April 1991.	Scheduled to start auctioning treasury bills in 1992.	Reserve requirement of 10 percent.	In mid-1991, steps were taken to improve the flexibility and effectiveness of bank-specific credit ceilings; ceilings abolished in late 1991.	To households, exporters, and agriculture.

Source: IMF staff.

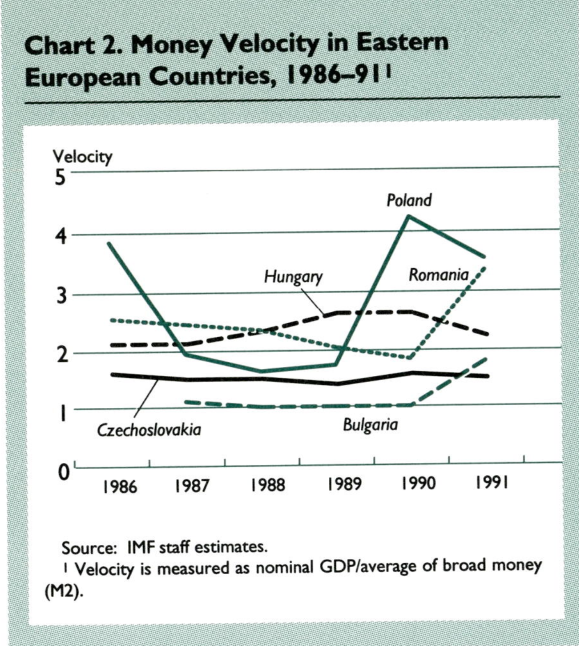

Chart 2. Money Velocity in Eastern European Countries, 1986–91[1]

Source: IMF staff estimates.
[1] Velocity is measured as nominal GDP/average of broad money (M2).

Similarly, because financial markets are evolving, there are uncertainties about the monetary policy transmission mechanism. As interest rates have been raised from levels that were strongly negative in real terms, transmission channels have been changing from predominantly direct credit rationing to a mixture of direct and price rationing through interest rates. (Even in fully liberalized economies, variations in the availability of credit have been considered an important transmission channel for the effects of monetary policy (Bernanke, 1983).) In this regard, the key market is that for bank reserves, which the authorities attempt to influence by controlling the stocks of banks' reserve balances. The term structure of interest rates also becomes an important aspect of the transmission of monetary policy because financial reforms are likely to affect the relationship between short- and long-term rates.

Third, in the PCPEs that have begun to rely on reserve requirements for controlling bank portfolios, the requirements have often been onerous, resulting in high effective taxation on intermediation through the banking system. Although this burden could be alleviated through the gradual reduction of reserve requirements, or the payment of interest on mandatory reserves, such an action could have adverse fiscal implications. At the same time, in several countries, the requirements for different types of deposits vary, which distorts relative rates paid on them, and gives an advantage to institutions with a particular specialization.[17]

Fiscal Policy

The financing of the public sector has undergone profound changes during the last two years. Instead of relying overwhelmingly on taxes on the enterprise sector (turnover and profits taxes), countries are moving toward policies—and introducing the appropriate framework—that will generate fiscal revenues from a much wider base.[18] The key issues that arise in the context of financial sector reforms relate to the financing of deficits. Until the transition toward market reforms began in earnest in the late 1980s, deficits (relative to GDP) tended to be small and cyclical. They were financed domestically, mostly with credit from the banking system. Nonbank financing was minimal because there was no domestic capital market and because financial assets were not available. In a centrally planned economy, bank financing does not have the same impact as in a market economy. However, bank financing of much higher budget deficits has continued in the last two to three years and, in the wake of recent reforms, has led to monetary expansion with the same adverse inflationary consequences as in other market economies (Tanzi, 1992).

The scale of future nonbank financing of fiscal deficits depends, in part, on domestic interest rates. Interest rates are being fully liberalized; the risks and uncertainties associated with the transition and the increasing demands on domestic savings by the private sector are likely to raise domestic real rates (to a level higher than international rates), which could increase the burden of noninflationary financing of deficits.

Generally, as the financial sector broadens and deepens, the financing of government deficits should become more efficient. Governments will then be in a position to smooth out temporary fluctuations in revenues and expenditures by being able to borrow the required funds on favorable terms from a wide variety of sources. Furthermore, the possibility of temporary borrowing should help with policy credibility in the sense that governments will not need to monetize deficits in cases of temporary shortfalls. For the financial sector itself, the availability of government paper with differing

---

[17]However, the reserve ratios might be expected to reflect that different degrees of risk are attached to different maturities.

[18]For a detailed discussion of the issues, see Tanzi (1990 and 1991).

maturity profiles can provide an important tool for removing significant mismatches between its assets and liabilities.

If the tax and expenditure systems are not flexible enough to permit rapid fiscal adjustment, some resort to inflation tax may be unavoidable. Then, the stage of development of the financial sector can have implications for collection of such a tax. That is, by providing a wide menu of assets and increasing flexibility, a highly developed financial sector may complicate the financing of fiscal deficits in the short run. For instance, although a reduction in reserve requirements during the development of the financial sector would reduce interest rate spreads, it could also reduce the base for the seigniorage tax. A reduced tax base implies that, to obtain any given level of tax revenues, the rate of inflation has to be higher than it would be if the required reserve ratio were high. To the extent that the public can anticipate higher inflation, investors will demand inflation premiums for lending to the government. Of course, any development that leads to a decline in the domestic tax base for seigniorage can have this adverse effect.

Another fiscal policy issue is the importance of using budgetary expenditures, rather than lending through the banking system, to support state enterprises with short-term financing needs. To the extent that such support is needed to provide incentives for enterprises to adjust, or to ward off hardship in the short run so that political support for the restructuring effort is not lost, going through the banking system will only lead to more nonperforming loans. It would be more appropriate to go through the budget, where the magnitude of the support is transparent.

Exchange Rate Policy and Convertibility

The choice of exchange rate regimes and currency convertibility are discussed in Borensztein and Masson (Part II of this Occasional Paper). The discussion below briefly summarizes only those aspects that are related to the development of the financial sector and the conduct of monetary policy. The PCPEs have adopted a range of exchange rate regimes, from a free float, as in Bulgaria, to a fixed but adjustable peg to a basket of major currencies, as in Poland. A stable exchange rate provides an anchor for nominal prices and, provided government policies are credible, may dampen inflationary expectations. It can also help reduce the riskiness of trade. But the equilibrium level at which the currency should be pegged can

be difficult to determine and, more important, its maintenance could require tight financial and fiscal policies (Aghevli, Khan, and Montiel, 1991). The budgetary difficulties outlined above and the problems that further tightening of monetary policy can create for enterprises and the banks may mean that the requisite policies cannot be readily implemented. In any case, if the initial stock of international reserves is inadequate, it may not be possible to peg the rate.

A floating rate regime would allow an additional degree of freedom but could adversely affect production and trade by increasing risk. At the same time, it would necessitate another nominal anchor, say, the money supply, but the incomplete development of money markets and shifts in the money demand and supply functions make the relationship between indirect control instruments and monetary targets uncertain. To the extent that this incomplete development, in turn, leads countries to rely on a system of bank-specific credit ceilings, credit allocation will be distorted. As a result, credit may be rationed away from firms that are likely to be profitable toward others that may be insolvent.

The reform of the financial sector also has an important bearing on current account convertibility, that is, access to foreign exchange for current account purposes. All Eastern European countries have moved quickly toward convertibility (Poland in 1990 and other countries in 1991), and this has been a major step forward in integrating these economies into the international economic system. In the absence of trade restrictions, current account convertibility subjects domestic producers to competition from abroad and confronts them with rational relative prices. In most of these economies, enterprises have a high degree of market power; thus, external competition can be an important spur to improving efficiency and can provide guidance for allocations of investment resources. The move toward convertibility also reflects the authorities' confidence in the reform process and enlarges consumption opportunities for individuals.

However, if convertibility is to be sustained, enterprises must have both the ability and the incentive to restructure production. If restructuring does not occur, these countries might have to rely heavily on restrictive macroeconomic policies or turn to restricting trade. In this respect, the improvement in some countries in the current accounts over the last two years should be seen in the context of other macroeconomic policies. For example, direct ceilings on commercial bank credit, combined with wage controls and the declines in real incomes, subdued imports and increased the supply of exports. As incomes and imports recover, convertibility can only be maintained if exports increase rapidly enough, which requires availability of credit on terms that are not onerous to potential exporters and adequate incentive.

In general, domestic supply problems arising from weakness in the banking and payments system and inter-enterprise arrears, as well as from inadequate incentives, could weaken the supply response and thus impair enterprises' ability to meet import competition and move further into export markets. Until the reform process was initiated, producers did not find it necessary to develop a marketing infrastructure because of the underlying pattern of trade and its concentration in foreign trade organizations. At the same time, guaranteed exports in the context of bilateral trade arrangements undermined incentives to improve the quality of manufactured goods. The transformation of production structures and the reorientation and entry into new markets require considerable new investment, so that enterprises are able to realize their potential comparative advantage. The reforms in the financial and enterprise sectors, which would lead to an increase in savings and in their allocation to the most optimal uses, are thus critical in maintaining convertibility, with all its attendant benefits.

Capital account convertibility, when introduced, should encourage an inflow of foreign savings into the PCPEs. In particular, it would provide incentives for an increased flow of foreign direct investment, which could also help bring in much-needed technological and managerial resources. Restricting capital account convertibility can cause distortions in the allocation of capital and weaken a potential disciplinary force on monetary policy. In any case, experience in other countries has shown that, with current account convertibility, capital controls are largely ineffective in an unstable economic environment.

However, to the extent that current account convertibility permits repatriation of earnings from foreign investment, this may be enough to encourage its inflow, and additional benefits in this regard may be limited. Capital convertibility might also interfere with the implementation of monetary policy, given that indirect instruments are still being developed. In particular, the PCPEs may not be regarded as having the requisite instruments to deal with short-term speculative capital movements, which could result from such convertibility. Finally, if the impact of changes in monetary policies on monetary aggregates and interest rates cannot be gauged, capital account convertibility could aggravate instability.

This section discusses issues related to promoting stability in the banking system and examines some of the pitfalls that are inherent in the reform process. The strength of the emerging market-oriented payments system of the PCPEs depends on the stability of the banking system. A stable banking system would enhance the financial intermediation process, which, in turn, could lead to an improvement in the savings performance as well as to a more efficient allocation of investment resources.

Confidence Building

In some cases, the impact of the reform process can be destabilizing. For instance, as long as banks still have a large portion of loans at fixed rates—all made when interest rates were much lower—freeing deposit rates would aggravate the already poor quality of their portfolios.[19] Even where the reform process does not exacerbate instability and, hence, undermine credibility, steps should be taken to establish confidence in the system. To promote confidence, the PCPEs need to hasten the implementation of banking laws and regulations that set the ground rules for bank operations and that constrain excessive risk taking. They can do this by designating the types of activities in which banks can engage, the types of loans and investments they can make, and the amount of capital they must maintain.

The supervisory process has a key role to play in establishing confidence. If supervision is not adequate, or if there are gaps in it, confidence in the banking system could be undermined. Although this is true of any country, it is critical in the reform environment of the PCPEs, which lack experience with the supervisory process. Foreign expertise may be required to train supervisory staff to identify problems before they reach proportions that ultimately cause failures and entail large costs. But the supervisory process will be particularly difficult because it may not be possible to distinguish between liquidity and solvency conditions, especially in light of the uncertainties regarding the banks' loan portfolios.

Deposit Protection Schemes

The development of the central banks and the enactment of the requisite banking legislation in the PCPEs must be seen as important steps toward establishing public confidence in the banking system. Credit extended by a central bank acting as lender of last resort to threatened banks can forestall, or offset, contractionary impulses, whereas reserve requirements and prudential supervision are designed to reduce the probability of similarly undesirable effects arising from unexpected deposit withdrawals or default losses on loans.

Nevertheless, the danger that bank illiquidity and bank runs will spill over to other banks (or cause negative confidence externalities) raises the question of how central banks can reduce potential effects of shifts on the confidence of depositors. Although the central bank's role as lender of last resort can combat such effects, the monetary authorities may have to take further steps to reduce systemic risk.

One method is suggested by the central banks' response to problem banks in other countries. If a commercial bank encounters illiquidity problems and possible insolvency, the regulatory authorities may decide to restructure the bank (or arrange a merger) and protect depositors at government expense. Such ad hoc interventions can create the presumption elsewhere in the banking system that a form of deposit insurance is in effect. This

---

[19]In Bulgaria, for example, a large portion of loans to enterprises was fixed at a low nominal rate, and parliamentary approval was required before the terms of the loans could be renegotiated. Pending approval, the net worth of the banking sector has declined sharply. A parallel can be drawn with the U.S. savings and loan debacle; in the early 1980s, when U.S. deposit rates were freed, the savings and loan industry had 80 percent of its assets in the form of fixed-rate loans, made when interest rates were much lower. This led to a decline in the industry's net worth, from around $30 billion at the end of 1980 to $4 billion two years later.

approach appears to provide considerable leeway to the monetary authorities in choosing deposit protection; however, it has distinct drawbacks. First, there is the problem of moral hazard, common to all forms of deposit insurance, which is discussed further below. Second, there may be uncertainty as to the extent to which this implicit deposit insurance will be provided in the event that banking difficulties take place on a larger scale in the future.

An explicit deposit insurance system is in place in a number of industrial countries as well as in some developing countries, including Chile, Colombia, and Kenya. The advantage of this system is that the amount of protection offered, the types of financial institutions and deposits that would be eligible, and the funding of the system are predetermined and are designed expressly to ease fears of banking system "contagion." The administrative process for handling failing banks and for protecting depositors can be eased because it is based on established rules and procedures and will produce relatively consistent outcomes over time.

The problems of moral hazard arise in both presumptive and explicit deposit insurance schemes, but for the PCPEs the difficulties inherent in the financial reform process are likely to send conflicting signals. The authorities may face systemic risk, but they also have to restructure the banks to make them responsive to market signals. Deposit insurance would continue to insulate depositors in PCPEs in that they assume little risk in their choice of financial institution, while the problem with regard to individual banks is to reform the credit process (so that the cost and availability of credit reflect the risks involved), which deposit insurance may tend to undermine.

A country considering an explicit deposit insurance scheme would have to address the problems that other countries have encountered in operating them, such as the adequacy of insurance premiums and the need to ensure partial risk sharing. Moreover, a number of recent studies have pointed to the problem that arises if an explicit insurance scheme is adopted when the existing financial sector is relatively weak (Talley and Mas, 1990). Because the banking systems are already under stress in the PCPEs, explicit insurance schemes could end up imposing large losses on insurance funds. These studies conclude that explicit schemes should be considered only after the first lines of defense against banking crises have been established. Until these conditions are met, countries should concentrate on ensuring that the central bank can effectively fulfill its traditional functions in the form of credit operations and banking regulation and supervision. In the near term, therefore, the restructuring and adequate capitalization of the banks in the PCPEs (which may involve presumptive deposit protection) must take priority over deposit insurance schemes designed to reduce subsequent systemic risk.

VIII   Summary and Conclusions

This section summarizes some of the key issues that have emerged in the preceding discussion and notes the constraints on achieving efficient financial intermediation in the previously centrally planned economies of Eastern Europe.

The stabilization policies and the structural reforms the PCPEs are pursuing have been accompanied by sharp declines in output. There are several reasons for the decline; however, inadequate provision of credit owing to unexpected price pressures and underdeveloped financial markets played a role in a number of countries. For financial markets to develop, the PCPEs must not only create the requisite institutions but also change the environment in which these institutions can operate. Despite favorable developments in several of the countries, a number of serious weaknesses remain, in particular, that of poor bank loan portfolios. This problem threatens the entire reform process. The PCPEs have several options for dealing with it, including writing off bad loans, monetary reform, and increasing loan-loss provisions through higher profitability.

Even if banks' balance sheets are cleaned, efficient banking operations will be hampered by a lack of criteria for judging the creditworthiness of enterprises as long as enterprises continue to be subject to soft budget constraints. In this respect, bank restructuring should be accompanied by the financial restructuring and subsequent privatization of enterprises. The banking sector is highly concentrated partly because commercial banks have only recently been instituted and partly because of the uncertainty caused by the transformation process. Lack of competition can lead to inefficiencies in the system and, although it may also lead to higher profitability in the short run, higher interest rates would adversely affect investment and lead to a further accumulation of bad loans.

The development of capital markets, in particular, the equity market, can play a useful role in the structural transformation process and can be hastened through privatization. Because these markets can complement the banking sector, they should be developed relatively quickly. However, the role of banks in the privatization process should be treated with caution. The PCPEs should ensure that the regulatory framework for the equity markets has transparency in the transactions and price-setting mechanism and precludes insider trading and other related practices.

In pursuing macroeconomic stabilization policies during the transition to market economies, the PCPEs must recognize that transmission mechanisms may not be fully developed. In particular, excessively restrictive monetary policies may aggravate output declines. Developing the financial sector may have important beneficial effects on fiscal policy.

A key prerequisite for establishing confidence in the banking systems is the institution of prudential regulation. In the short run, however, the restructuring and adequate capitalization of the banks should take priority over instituting explicit deposit protection schemes.

Appendix   Corporate Financing Patterns: Some Illustrative Evidence

There are two sources of information on corporate financing patterns in the industrial and developing countries. The first is national flow-of-funds accounts, which provide records of flows between different sectors of an economy and between domestic and overseas residents. The relevant accounts for the financing pattern are the flows to and from the nonfinancial companies, and the data discussed below for the industrial countries are derived from this source. The second source is individual company accounts, which are aggregated across companies to provide an indication of overall financing patterns. The data discussed below for the developing countries are derived from this source. In theory, flow-of-funds statistics provide comprehensive coverage of transactions between sectors as company accounts are usually only available for a sample of a country's total corporate sector. However, the data in company accounts are usually more reliable than in flow-of-funds accounts. It is important to note, however, that either source of data yields much the same broad conclusions with respect to the average corporate financing patterns for industrial countries. Therefore, comparisons between the sets of industrial and developing countries will not necessarily be inappropriate.

Appendix Table 1 provides the average financing proportions for the seven largest industrial countries on a gross and a net basis, averaged over the period 1970 to 1985.[20] Data on a gross basis show the sources of funds used by the nonfinancial corporate sector, including internal funds (retentions) and external funds. The latter category consists largely of funds from the capital market, including the securities markets (short-term securities, bonds, and equities) and the nonsecurities markets (bank loans). Data on a net basis exclude the corporate sector's deposits to banks, equities redeemed during the period, and so on, and allows a breakdown of corporate growth (in physical assets and stocks) to be ascribed to different sources of finance.

Three main points emerge from Appendix Table 1. First, corporate growth is financed largely from internal sources. Thus, on a net basis, retained profits accounted for more than 100 percent of finance for all nonfinancial companies in the United Kingdom and for over 85 percent for the United States. In Italy, with the lowest proportion, over half of investment in physical assets and stocks is funded from retentions.

Second, in most countries companies raise a limited amount of finance from the securities markets. Companies in the United States raised the largest amount at 13 percent; those in Germany and the United Kingdom raised negative net amounts from the markets. In particular, the share of equities markets is small, with the new share issues accounting for less than 5 percent of total finance raised in five of the seven countries. In the United Kingdom, equities made a negative contribution (indicating that the value of shares redeemed, largely on account of takeovers, was greater than the amount raised by corporate new issues).

Third, bank loans play an important role, particularly in France, Italy, and Japan. On a gross basis, the contribution of bank loans to corporate finance in west Germany is no different from that in the United Kingdom and the United States. It is also worth noting that, as the figures for trade credits indicate, overall nonfinancial enterprises are suppliers of credit to other sectors, in particular to consumers.

A number of explanations can account for the above features of industrial country corporate finance, relating to the cost of credit, its availability, and so on. One key explanation, which points to the incompleteness of markets and contracts, emphasizes the relationship between corporate finance and corporate control. The contention is that external intervention is costly because owners, or creditors, are either poor managers or difficult to organize; thus, internal finance dominates. This explanation may be particularly appropriate for the United Kingdom and the United States, where the separation between management and finance is marked. Furthermore, creditors that are dispersed

---

[20]The data are obtained from Mayer (1989), Tables 1 and 3.

Table 1. Large Industrial Countries: Financing of Nonfinancial Enterprises, 1970–85

A. In percent of total financing

	Canada	France	Germany	Italy	Japan	United Kingdom	United States
Internal finance	54.2	44.1	55.2	38.5	33.7	72.0	66.9
External finance	45.8	55.9	44.8	61.5	66.3	28.0	33.1
Of which:							
Loans	12.8	41.5	21.1	38.6	40.7	21.4	23.1
Trade credit	8.6	4.7	2.2	—	18.3	2.8	8.4
Bonds	6.1	2.3	0.7	2.4	3.1	0.8	9.7
Short-term securities	1.4	—	—	0.1	—	2.3	1.4
Equities	11.9	10.6	2.1	10.8	3.5	4.9	0.8
Other	4.9	−3.3	18.6	9.6	0.7	−4.2	−10.1

B. In percent of net investment expenditure

	Canada	France	Germany	Italy	Japan	United Kingdom	United States
Internal finance	76.4	61.4	70.9	51.9	59.9	102.4	85.9
External finance	23.6	38.6	29.1	48.1	42.1	−2.4	14.1
Of which:							
Loans	15.2	37.3	12.1	27.7	50.4	7.6	24.4
Trade credit	−4.4	−0.6	−2.1	—	−11.2	−1.1	−1.4
Bonds	8.5	1.6	−1.0	1.6	2.1	−1.1	11.6
Short-term securities	−0.6	−0.1	−0.1	−1.3	—	1.7	0.4
Equities	2.5	6.3	0.6	8.2	4.6	−3.3	1.1
Other	−2.4	−5.8	19.5	11.9	−3.8	−6.1	−22.0

Source: Mayer (1989).

and difficult to organize play an especially small role. Finance will be provided instead by intermediaries that are closely integrated into their corporate sectors, as in France, Italy, and Japan.

Appendix Table 2 presents the pattern of corporate finance in the developing countries. The data are based on the company accounts of the top 50 manufacturing companies quoted on the stock market of each country. Although the sample is limited, it is estimated that these companies account for a substantial portion, often more than half, of the output in the nonfinancial corporate sector in these countries. The main points that emerge from this table are the following:

First, although the structure of corporate finance varies widely among the developing countries, the use of external finance is far greater than in the industrial countries. For instance, the average share of external finance was almost 80 percent in Jordan, Korea, and Turkey and close to 60 percent in all the other countries except Malaysia.

Second, in more than half the countries in the sample, the companies used much more equity

Table 2. Selected Developing Countries: Financing of Nonfinancial Enterprises, 1980–88

(Percent of net investment expenditure)

Country	Internal Financing	External Financing		
		Total	Equity	Debt
India	34.9	65.1	14.0	51.1
Jordan	11.6	88.4	46.6	41.8
Korea	21.0	79.0	44.3	34.6
Malaysia	66.8	33.2	14.9	18.3
Mexico	26.3	73.7	69.4	4.3
Pakistan	42.0	58.0	20.4	37.6
Thailand	24.1	75.9	40.9	35.0
Turkey	17.5	82.6	60.9	21.7
Zimbabwe	42.9	57.1	35.2	21.9

Source: Singh and Hamid (1992).

than debt to finance the growth of net assets. In Mexico, Turkey, and Zimbabwe, equity issues

Table 3. Selected Developing Countries: Equity Market Concentration
(In percent of total)

Market Share	Share of Total Market Capitalization Held by Ten Largest Stocks, end-1990	Share of Value Traded by Ten Most Active Stocks, end-1990
Latin America		
Argentina	60.2	73.7
Brazil	22.4	34.4
Chile	48.8	56.7
Colombia	76.9	38.5
Mexico	35.5	25.7
Venezuela	60.9	86.6
East Asia		
Korea	30.9	25.6
Philippines	56.3	56.0
Taiwan Province of China	53.9	20.2
South Asia		
India	23.5	30.6
Indonesia	51.0	41.1
Malaysia	28.0	19.2
Pakistan	25.5	20.2
Thailand	35.7	20.4
Europe/Mideast/Africa		
Greece	48.2	57.4
Jordan	67.2	46.8
Nigeria	53.1	60.7
Portugal	46.6	23.8
Turkey	61.7	40.0
Zimbabwe	48.3	33.5
Industrial country markets		
Canada	28.4	. . .
France	25.8	. . .
Germany	41.7	. . .
Japan	17.1	. . .
Switzerland	49.6	. . .
United Kingdom	24.4	. . .
United States	14.1	. . .

Source: International Finance Corporation (1991).

accounted for a far greater proportion of external finance than did debt issues.[21] This pattern of external finance contrasts sharply with the pattern noted for the industrial countries.

It could, however, be argued that the results for the developing countries are biased because the sample includes only the largest firms. Although this is possible, there is some evidence that, even if only the largest firms in the United Kingdom or the United States are considered, the differences in the financing patterns will still persist. Singh and Hamid (1992) also note that firms in industrial countries relied much more heavily on external equity finance at an earlier stage in their development. In this respect, it could be argued that the developing country corporate financing pattern is now following a similar evolutionary path.

---

[21]At the same time, there was a very high concentration in equity holdings (see Appendix Table 3).

References

Aghevli, Bijan B., Eduardo Borensztein, and Tessa van der Willigen, *Stabilization and Structural Reform in the Czech and Slovak Federal Republic: First Stage*, Occasional Paper 92 (Washington: International Monetary Fund, March 1992).

Aghevli, Bijan B., Mohsin S. Khan, and Peter J. Montiel, *Exchange Rate Policy in Developing Countries: Some Analytical Issues*, Occasional Paper 78 (Washington: International Monetary Fund, March 1991).

Bernanke, Ben S., "Nonmonetary Effects of the Financial Crisis in the Propagation of the Great Depression," NBER Working Paper No. 1054 (Cambridge, Massachusetts: National Bureau of Economic Research, January 1983).

Blanchard, Oliver, and others, *Reform in Eastern Europe* (Cambridge, Massachusetts: MIT Press, 1991).

Blejer, Mario I., and Silvia B. Sagari, "Hungary: The Initial Stages in the Financial Sector Reform of a Socialist Economy in Transition," *Applied Financial Economics*, Vol. 2 (March 1992), pp. 33–42.

Boote, Anthony R., and Janos Somogyi, *Economic Reform in Hungary Since 1968*, Occasional Paper 83 (Washington: International Monetary Fund, July 1991).

Borensztein, Eduardo, and Manmohan S. Kumar, "Proposals for Privatization in Eastern Europe," *Staff Papers*, International Monetary Fund, Vol. 38 (June 1991), pp. 300–326.

Borensztein, Eduardo, and Paul R. Masson, "Exchange Arrangements of the Previously Centrally Planned Economies" (Part II of this Occasional Paper).

Borensztein, Eduardo, and Peter Montiel, "Savings, Investment, and Growth in Eastern Europe," IMF Working Paper 91/61 (Washington: International Monetary Fund, June 1991).

Brainard, Lawrence J., "Strategies for Economic Transformation in Central and Eastern Europe: Role of Financial Market Reform," in *Transformation of Planned Economies*, ed. by Hans Blommestein and Michael Marrese (Paris: Organization for Economic Cooperation and Development, 1991), pp. 95–108.

Bruno, Michael, and Leora Meridor, "The Costly Transition from Stabilization to Sustainable Growth: Israel's Case," in *Lessons of Economic Stabilization and Its Aftermath*, ed. by Bruno and others (Cambridge, Massachusetts: MIT Press, 1991).

Bruno, Michael, and others, eds., *Lessons of Economic Stabilization and Its Aftermath* (Cambridge, Massachusetts: MIT Press, 1991).

Calvo, Guillermo A., and Fabrizio Coricelli, "Stabilizing a Previously Centrally Planned Economy: Poland 1990," *Economic Policy: A European Forum* (April 1992), pp. 176–226.

Calvo, Guillermo A., and Jacob A. Frenkel (1991a), "From Centrally Planned to Market Economy: The Road from CPE to PCPE," *Staff Papers*, International Monetary Fund, Vol. 38 (June), pp. 268–99.

———— (1991b), "Obstacles to Transforming Centrally Planned Economies: The Role of Capital Markets," in *The Transition to a Market Economy in Central and Eastern Europe*, ed. by P. Marer and S. Zecchini (Paris: Organization for Economic Cooperation and Development).

Calvo, Guillermo A., and Pablo E. Guidotti (1991a), "Interest Rates, Financial Structure, and Growth: Bolivia in a Comparative Perspective" (mimeographed; Washington: International Monetary Fund, May).

———— (1991b), "On the Flexibility of Monetary Policy: The Case of the Optimal Inflation Tax" (mimeographed; Washington: International Monetary Fund, October).

Dailami, Mansoor, and Marcelo Giugale, *Reflections on Credit Policy in Developing Countries: Its Effect on Private Investment*, Policy, Research, and External Affairs Working Paper WPS 654 (Washington: World Bank, April 1991).

Dailami, Mansoor, and Michael Atkin, *Stock Markets in Developing Countries: Key Issues and a Research Agenda*, Policy, Research, and External Affairs Working Paper WPS 515 (Washington: World Bank, October 1990).

Darrat, Ali, and Tarun Mukherjee, "Behavior of the Stock Market in a Developing Economy," *Economic Letters*, Vol. 22 (1986), pp. 273–78.

Demekas, Dimitri G., and Mohsin S. Khan, *The Romanian Economic Reform Program*, Occasional Paper 89 (Washington: International Monetary Fund, November 1991).

Diamond, Douglas W., "Monitoring and Reputation: The Choice between Bank Loans and Directly Placed Debt," *Journal of Political Economy*, Vol. 99 (August 1991), pp. 689–721.

Dornbusch, Rudiger, and Alejandro Reynoso, "Financial Factors in Economic Development," NBER Working Paper No. 2889 (Cambridge, Massachusetts: National Bureau of Economic Research, March 1989).

Dornbusch, Rudiger, and Holger Wolf, "Monetary Overhang and Reforms in the 1940s," NBER Working Paper No. 3456 (Cambridge, Massachusetts: National Bureau of Economic Research, October 1990).

Fischer, S., and R.C. Merton, "Macroeconomics and Finance: The Role of the Stock Market," in *Essays on Macroeconomic Implications of Financial and Labor Markets and Political Processes*, ed. by Karl Brunner and Allan H. Meltzer, Carnegie-Rochester Conference Series on Public Policy, Vol. 21 (New York; Amsterdam: North-Holland, 1984).

Fry, M., *Money, Interest, and Banking in Economic Development* (Baltimore: Johns Hopkins Press, 1988).

Gelb, Alan H., and Cheryl W. Gray, *The Transformation of Economies in Central and Eastern Europe: Issues, Progress, and Prospects*, Policy and Research Series No. 17 (Washington: World Bank, 1991).

Gilbert, R. Alton, "Bank Market Structure and Competition: A Survey," *Journal of Money, Credit and Banking*, Vol. 16 (November 1984), pp. 617–60.

Greene, Joshua E., and Peter Isard, *Currency Convertibility and the Transformation of Centrally Planned Economies*, Occasional Paper 81 (Washington: International Monetary Fund, June 1991).

Hardy, Daniel C., "Soft Budget Constraints, Firm Commitments and the Social Safety Net," *Staff Papers*, International Monetary Fund, Vol. 39 (June 1992), pp. 310–29.

Hughes, Gordon, and Paul Hare, "The International Competitiveness of Industries in Bulgaria, Czechoslovakia, Hungary, and Poland," paper presented at the European Economic Association Conference, Cambridge, England, September 1991.

International Finance Corporation (IFC), *Emerging Stock Markets: Factbook* (Washington: IFC, 1991).

Kenen, Peter B., "Transitional Arrangements for Trade and Payments Among the CMEA Countries," *Staff Papers*, International Monetary Fund, Vol. 38 (June 1991), pp. 235–67.

Khan, Mohsin S., and V. Sundararajan, "Financial Sector Reforms and Monetary Policy," IMF Working Paper 91/127 (Washington: International Monetary Fund, December 1991).

Kim, E.H., "Financing Korean Corporations: Evidence and Theory," in *Korean Economic Development*, ed. by J.K. Kim (New York: Greenwood Press, 1990).

Kolodko, Grzegorz, "Transition from Socialism and Stabilization Policies: The Polish Experience" (unpublished; Washington: International Monetary Fund, June 1991).

Kornai, Janos, "Soft Budget Constraint," *Kyklos*, Vol. 39 (1986), pp. 3–30.

Kumar, Manmohan S., *Growth, Acquisition and Investment: An Analysis of the Growth of Industrial Firms and Their Overseas Activities* (New York: Cambridge University Press, 1984).

Lane, Timothy, "Inflation Stabilization and Economic Transformation in Poland: The First Year," Carnegie-Rochester Conference Series on Public Policy, Vol. 36 (Amsterdam; New York: North-Holland, July 1992).

Leite, Sérgio Pereira, and V. Sundararajan, "Issues in Interest Rate Management and Liberalization," *Staff Papers*, International Monetary Fund, Vol. 37 (December 1990), pp. 735–52.

Long, Millard, and Silvia B. Sagari, *Financial Reform in Socialist Economies in Transition*, Policy, Research, and External Affairs Working Paper WPS 711 (Washington: World Bank, June 1991).

Luders, Rolf J., "Massive Divestiture and Privatization: Lessons from Chile," *Contemporary Policy Issues* (October 1991), pp. 1–19.

Mayer, Colin, *Myths of the West: Lessons from Developed Countries for Development Finance*, Policy, Planning, and Research Working Paper WPS 301 (Washington: World Bank, November 1989).

Ortiz, Guillermo, "Mexico beyond the Debt Crisis: Toward Sustainable Growth with Price Stability," in *Lessons of Economic Stabilization and Its Aftermath*, ed. by Bruno and others (Cambridge, Massachusetts: MIT Press, 1991).

Osband, Kent, "Index Number Biases During Price Liberalization," *Staff Papers*, International Monetary Fund, Vol. 39 (June 1992), pp. 287–309.

Sachs, Jeffrey, "Accelerating Privatization in Eastern Europe: The Case of Poland," Working Paper No. 92, World Institute for Development Economics Research, United Nations University (September 1991).

Singh, Ajit, and Javed Hamid, *Corporate Financial Structures in Developing Countries*, IFC Technical Paper No. 1 (Washington: World Bank, 1992).

Sundararajan, V., "Financial Sector Reform and Central Banking in Centrally Planned Economies," IMF Working Paper 90/120 (Washington: International Monetary Fund, December 1990).

Sundararajan, V., and Tomas J. Baliño, eds., *Banking Crises: Cases and Issues* (Washington: International Monetary Fund, 1991).

Talley, Samuel H., and Ignacio Mas, "Deposit Insurance in Developing Countries," *Finance and Development*, International Monetary Fund and World Bank, Vol. 27 (December 1990), pp. 43–45.

Tanzi, Vito, "Fiscal Issues in Economies in Transition," paper presented at the World Bank Conference on Adjustment and Growth: Lessons for Eastern Europe (The Conference, 1990).

——————, "Tax Reform in Economies in Transition: A Brief Introduction to the Main Issues," IMF Working Paper 91/23 (Washington: International Monetary Fund, March 1991).

——————, ed., *Fiscal Policies in Economies in Transition* (Washington: International Monetary Fund, 1992).

Volcker, Paul, "The Role of Central Banks," in *Central Banking Issues in Emerging Market-Oriented Economies: A Symposium* (Kansas City, Missouri: Federal Reserve Bank of Kansas City, 1990).

Williamson, John, *The Economic Opening of Eastern Europe* (Washington: Institute for International Economics, May 1991).

Part II

Exchange Arrangements of Previously Centrally Planned Economies

I Introduction

The reforms undertaken by the previously centrally planned economies (PCPEs) of Eastern Europe[1] in their transition to market economies are unprecedented in scale. A central aspect of the reforms has been the integration of these countries into the international monetary and trading system. Now that several Eastern European economies have experienced more than one year of reform, following a variety of approaches, it seems useful to survey some general aspects of their choices of exchange arrangement. It is hoped that the analysis may help to inform the choices of other PCPEs that are less advanced in the reform process—in particular, the states of the former U.S.S.R., which are not, however, discussed in the paper.

There is a considerable body of literature on the exchange arrangements of market economies, whether industrial or developing countries.[2] Although this literature provides insights that are useful for PCPEs, these countries have unique features that condition their choices of exchange arrangement. To begin with, these economies suffer from enormous price distortions, with prices independent of market forces and with shortages of goods; lack of competition because production by state firms was based on a high degree of specialization; and a monetary overhang associated with the absence of monetary control. Price liberalization is, therefore, likely to imply an initial jump in the price level and potentially large relative price movements. Also important for the design of reform is the political context created by the rapid abandonment of control over all aspects of economic life by a one-party state in favor of democratic pluralism and a market-based system, with the consequent need to build institutions virtually from scratch. Another aspect is the external context of these economies: until recently, they traded extensively with each other[3] but very little with the rest of the world. Consequently, they typically begin the reform process with low levels of foreign exchange reserves.

These features of the PCPEs make it especially important for them to liberalize their exchange rate systems and to open up their economies to foreign trade in order to import financial discipline, provide competition for domestic producers, and establish an anchor for domestic prices. Access to foreign currency for current account purposes—that is, current account convertibility—is a significant part of the reform process. In this context, a fixed exchange rate can also contribute to stabilizing prices and providing a nominal anchor. However, the goal of price stability has to be balanced against the need to maintain competitiveness and to prevent large payments imbalances, which may require a more flexible exchange arrangement. It must also be recognized that choices of exchange rate arrangement are conditioned by the nature of policymaking institutions. If financial discipline cannot be achieved, then an unchanged peg to a stable currency cannot be maintained. To differing extents, the PCPEs will be constrained by budgetary pressures and lack of central bank credibility and independence, as well as by a shortage of foreign exchange reserves. Insofar as the structure of their economies will determine their choice of exchange arrangement, it is likely that no single type of exchange rate arrangement will be appropriate for all the PCPEs.

Another difficulty inherent in the transition to market economies is how to proceed as quickly as possible toward reform and yet moderate the adjustment costs of a rapid shift away from traditional production patterns, which were largely the result of the arbitrary choices of central planners. The risk that a sharp decline in trade among the PCPEs will produce large declines in output is very high, given the extent of interdependence; indeed,

---

[1] In this paper, Eastern Europe will be taken to comprise Bulgaria, the Czech and Slovak Federal Republic, Hungary, Poland, and Romania. The experience of other countries in the region (Albania, the former GDR, and Yugoslavia) will not be discussed here.

[2] See, for example, Aghevli, Khan, and Montiel (1991) and Frenkel, Goldstein, and Masson (1991).

[3] In particular, the countries of Eastern Europe with the former U.S.S.R., and the states of the former U.S.S.R. among themselves.

this has already occurred during the past year, partly because of the dismantling of the payments arrangements of the former Council for Mutual Economic Assistance (CMEA) linking the countries of Central and Eastern Europe and the former U.S.S.R.

This paper analyzes these issues by examining the different exchange arrangements as they apply to PCPEs and the lessons to be drawn from the experience of Eastern Europe. Section II examines general arguments for convertibility in the PCPEs, while Section III considers the desirable degree of exchange rate flexibility. Section IV examines the experience of the countries of Eastern Europe. Section V presents conclusions.

II Currency Convertibility

Convertibility of domestic into foreign currencies is an extremely important aspect of the reform process for the PCPEs because it helps them to move to world market prices and thereby to become competitive. However, unrestricted convertibility is likely to take time to achieve; at least initially, convertibility is likely to be limited to current transactions. Requirements for convertibility and the desired speed of the transition are discussed in the following section.[4]

Current Account Convertibility

Full (or unrestricted) convertibility of a currency is defined by Haberler (1954) in the following terms: "any holder of any national currency should be free to exchange it at the ruling rate of exchange (which may be either constant or variable) into any other currency." In practice, reforming economies are likely to aim for a more limited objective—the freedom to exchange currencies for current account transactions. The obligations of Article VIII of the IMF's Articles of Agreement pertain to current account convertibility.[5] In particular, members may not, without the approval of the IMF, inter alia, impose restrictions on the making of payments and transfers in connection with foreign trade in goods and services, interest on loans and investment income, a moderate amount of amortization, or moderate remittances for family living expenses, nor may they engage in multiple currency practices.[6]

Current account convertibility subjects domestic producers to competition from abroad and thereby invokes a system of rational relative prices, at least for tradable goods and provided trade restrictions are not imposed (Polak, 1991). In economies where prices have been administered and where existing cost structures do not guide relative prices because decisions to invest and produce were not made on the basis of maximizing profits or even of covering costs,[7] import prices provide an invaluable guide to rational pricing. Moreover, in recently liberalized economies with large enterprises and small domestic markets, where domestic competition is unlikely to operate, opening up the economy to foreign competition is especially important. It is important to establish early in the reform process markets that allow for the free influence of world prices in order to shift resources to sectors that reflect comparative advantage and also because investment—in both physical and human capital—involves long lead times.

It is clear that restrictions on trade can interfere with these forces even if payments restrictions are removed: although they are logically separate, and responsibility for them is divided between the IMF and the General Agreement on Tariffs and Trade (GATT), it is necessary to consider the two aspects together (Gilman, 1990 and Polak, 1991). Convertibility does not require complete trade liberalization, but some forms of restriction are particularly inimical to the operation of competition described above. Tariffs, especially if kept to moderate levels and uniform across goods, are preferable to quantitative restrictions. They are more transparent, allow the effect of world relative prices to operate, and provide fiscal revenue. Resources are better allocated on the basis of price, rather than nonprice rationing. Quantitative restrictions, if binding, not only impose no discipline at the margin but also arbitrarily allocate scarcity rents to those granted import permits.[8]

---

[4]Convertibility in the context of Eastern Europe is discussed extensively by Greene and Isard (1991). Other references include Williamson (1991a, 1991b).

[5]For a discussion of the concept of convertibility in the Articles, see Gold (1971).

[6]Article VIII, sections 2 and 3, and Article XXX(*d*).

[7]McKinnon (1991) argues that when inputs and outputs are valued at world prices, a large proportion of production in Eastern Europe and the former U.S.S.R. may result in negative value added.

[8]The European Payments Union had as one of its primary goals the elimination of quantitative restrictions on trade. Its success helped achieve de facto convertibility for most member countries in 1958.

There is also a linkage between convertibility and the choice of exchange rate regime. Determining the exchange rate in a free market requires the existence of convertibility because giving access to such a market is the same as granting the right to exchange domestic for foreign currency. It may, indeed, be difficult in such circumstances to restrict the purpose for which the foreign exchange is acquired, in particular, to limit convertibility to current transactions. A related issue is what exchange control regulations to impose. For instance, should residents be permitted to hold foreign currency balances or instead be obliged to surrender export receipts?[9] If they are allowed to hold foreign exchange, can they do so in banks abroad, or should they be forced to repatriate these balances and hold them domestically? Must foreign exchange transactions be centralized at the central bank? Absence of restrictions may facilitate capital flight, but monitoring and enforcement may be difficult. A detailed discussion of exchange control regulations goes beyond the scope of this paper.

Capital Account Convertibility

Like current account convertibility, capital account convertibility has the advantage of imposing world market prices, in particular, of channeling world savings to their most profitable uses and leading to equalization of the rate of return. To satisfy the investment needs of the PCPEs, it is important to attract foreign savings and to allocate them on a rate of return basis. However, two factors may make it less imperative to move to early and unrestricted capital account convertibility.

First, because current account convertibility already permits repatriation of earnings from foreign investment, it provides some inducement to capital inflows. Capital account convertibility need not be granted to residents in order to allow repatriation of foreign capital as well. Access to foreign exchange for capital exports could be granted to foreigners only and limited to funds brought into the country after a certain date.

Second, capital account convertibility might make the economy more vulnerable to speculative flows, which could be especially destabilizing in the early stages of reform when foreign exchange reserves are low, and the credibility of policymakers has yet to be established. On the one hand, capital flows might interfere with monetary policy

unless the central bank can sterilize them, and central banks are unlikely to have the instruments to do so initially. On the other hand, without capital account convertibility, the discipline imposed on monetary policy by capital flows would be lessened.

In any case, restricting capital account convertibility not only causes distortions but because it is difficult to monitor and enforce, it is unlikely to be completely effective. Therefore, it may be impracticable to allow convertibility for current transactions but not for capital account transactions. For instance, many countries—including a number in Latin America—have experienced capital flight despite controls on capital outflows.[10] Speculation against a currency may also manifest itself through "leads and lags" in settling trade flows.

Therefore, the PCPEs may have to accept some degree of capital account convertibility de facto. In these circumstances, sound monetary and fiscal policies become especially important insofar as they increase confidence and lower incentives for capital flight. In the presence of sound policies, restrictions on capital are unlikely to be necessary; on the contrary, their removal could increase the credibility of the authorities.

Speed of the Move to Convertibility and Preconditions for Its Success

Because of its role in reinforcing the liberalization process, current account convertibility should ideally be declared immediately along with a comprehensive set of reforms sufficient to establish the preconditions for convertibility. These preconditions include an appropriate exchange rate, adequate international liquidity, the absorption of any liquidity overhang, and sustained and sound macroeconomic policies.[11] There are dangers in moving to convertibility before these preconditions have been met.

First, the reform effort could lose credibility if a move to convertibility had to be reversed. Because the reform of the PCPEs takes place in a context of pervasive uncertainty about equilibrium prices and supply responses, doubts will necessarily remain as to whether the exchange rate is competitive and reserves are adequate. Convertibility at an exchange rate that lacks credibility is likely to provoke a surge of imports, at which point the authorities will be forced to choose between a sharp compression of demand or abandoning convertibility (Williamson, 1991b, p. 381). A policy trade-off is therefore involved in deciding how

---

[9]As Gold (1971) points out, current account convertibility as defined in the IMF's Articles does not rule out surrender requirements, which would forbid resident holdings of foreign currencies. Surrender requirements may be a means of ensuring that foreign currency is not used for capital account purposes.

[10]See Dooley (1988).

[11]See Greene and Isard (1991).

much time should be allowed for such uncertainty to dissipate.[12]

Second, a quick move to convertibility might require too great a depreciation of the real exchange rate if it were attempted early in the reform process (Nuti, 1991). The reason for this is that production has to be reoriented gradually toward goods that are salable on world markets; until that is done, there will be an incipient imbalance of imports over exports. Owing to the lack of portfolio diversification under central planning, there may also be a large pent-up demand for foreign assets, which capital controls may only partially repress. Unless foreign exchange reserves are available to pay for imports and to acquire foreign assets, a large exchange rate depreciation will be required for balance of payments equilibrium to be achieved; it is argued that this is undesirable because it will depress real incomes, undervalue domestic assets, lead to a contraction of domestic demand, and exacerbate inflationary pressures. The imbalance of trade, however, can be made manageable by tariffs and export subsidies, which, in principle, can substitute for the effects of exchange rate depreciation.[13] Furthermore, it is not clear whether the harmful effects of "over-depreciation" on real activity would be more serious than those resulting from lack of access to imported inputs and consumption goods. It is true that, unless the demand for a country's exports and the supply of its imports are infinitely elastic, an exchange rate depreciation would lead to a terms of trade deterioration with negative effects on domestic demand through lower real income.[14] However, if import restrictions prevented the exchange rate depreciation, the shadow price of imports would also rise, so that any properly calculated real income measure should fall as a result.

A *third* objection to rapid convertibility is that it may not be possible to put in place the institutions needed for implementing the supporting financial policies.[15] Enterprise reform takes time, and, during the transition period, enterprises are likely to continue to operate with soft budget constraints and to grant unrealistically high wage increases. This will show up in negative cash flows covered by inter-enterprise credits, pressure on the banking system to grant loans, or drains on government budgets. Monetary policy institutions will not yet have developed the instruments and experience to execute sound financial policies convincingly.[16] The tax system must be reformed in order to generate needed revenues and to prevent pressures for monetization. In this context, an attempt to maintain convertibility at a fixed exchange rate risks eventual overvaluation and ultimate abandonment of the exchange rate peg or a reversal of the liberalization to achieve payments balance. The alternative of frequent devaluations might weaken the credibility of the reform effort and add to, or at least accommodate, inflationary pressures. Similarly, an initial overdevaluation may build in wage and price pressures at the early stages of reform. The section below considers alternative degrees of exchange rate flexibility, depending on the emphasis given to the two objectives of achieving a nominal anchor and maintaining competitiveness.

The major objection to a quick move to current account convertibility thus seems to be concern about the adequacy of reserves or external financing when the equilibrium level of the exchange rate is not known, and about the ability of the authorities to put supporting policies in place fast enough. In the face of a deterioration in the terms of trade—for instance, owing to higher energy prices—if reserves are not adequate and exports cannot be expanded quickly enough, countries may be forced to make large cuts in imports, and governments may prefer not to allow markets to determine the allocation of scarce foreign exchange.

Even if there are sufficient reserves to make convertibility in trade with market economies possible, there may still be a case for trading with other PCPEs on a different basis because those trading partners have not themselves reached the stage of convertibility. One alternative would be to establish a regional payments union, an option not discussed here.

---

[12]The United Kingdom in 1947 is often cited as demonstrating a premature move to convertibility that had to be reversed within a little over a month because of rapid exhaustion of reserves. However, because the situation of the United Kingdom was complicated by the existence of large external sterling balances, it is not directly relevant for the PCPEs. Moreover, convertibility need not have involved a fixed exchange rate; convertibility of sterling at a floating rate was explored in the early 1950s (Kaplan and Schleiminger, 1989).

[13]There could be a fixed timetable for their removal so that investment could, in principle, look ahead to undistorted prices. It might be difficult, however, to precommit credibly to such a timetable.

[14]Akerlof and others (1991) argue that currency union caused a large negative aggregate demand shock in the former German Democratic Republic.

[15]Calvo and Frenkel (1991) stress the need to develop credit markets and discuss the vulnerability of reform to imperfect credibility.

[16]See Part I of this paper for a discussion of the magnitude of the institution-building task in this area.

III The Desirable Degree of Exchange Rate Flexibility

Exchange rate flexibility and fixity are relative terms. Choices of exchange rate regime range from (1) commitment to a fixed rate, such as that implied by currency union or a currency board;[17] (2) pegged but adjustable rates, where different frequencies of adjustment are possible; (3) a managed float; and (4) a freely floating rate. In practice, as discussed in Section IV, the exchange rate regimes of the Eastern European countries have generally fallen into categories (2) and (3).

The economic literature has identified several guidelines concerning the desirable degree of exchange rate flexibility, which depend on the structural characteristics of the economy, on the main type of shocks to which the economy is subjected, and on the reputation and credibility enjoyed by the authorities.[18] At the risk of oversimplification, these guidelines can be summarized as suggesting that less flexibility in the exchange rate is desirable when the economy is more open to international trade; when real wages are sticky, the most important shocks are of domestic and monetary origin, and domestic stabilization is given priority over the balance of payments; and when the government is able to impose strong financial discipline, and its policy actions enjoy sufficient credibility. The analyses that support these conclusions, however, have always been based on the conditions of well-established market economies in both industrial and developing countries. While the same general principles still offer useful guidelines for the reforming PCPEs, a number of new problems and objectives emerge in their case.

A most urgent objective for these economies in transition is to control the inflationary process that follows the liberalization of prices after decades of controls and distortions. Liberalization generates an initial price jump owing to existing shortages, the monetary overhang, and the increase in some key administered prices—notably of energy and food products. Price increases tend to persist as the higher costs of inputs work their way through the productive system, and partial or full indexation increases ceilings on wage increases. A stabilization policy is required to ensure that the rate of inflation converges downward to an acceptable level. Pegged exchange rates can help in the stabilization process, as discussed below, but they require adequate foreign exchange reserves; for many countries, initial reserve levels and external support are low, and the prospects for sustained external financing are open to question.

Advantages of Exchange Rate Stability

In both developing and industrial countries, exchange rate stability against a hard currency has been recognized as a useful instrument to aid in stabilization efforts. The exchange rate provides an anchor for nominal prices and—provided government policies are credible—acts as a device to dampen inflation expectations. For the specific conditions of PCPEs, exchange rate stability has the additional advantage of helping international prices provide a guide for market-clearing domestic prices.

After decades during which market forces were virtually ignored in price determination, there is considerable uncertainty about both the relative price structure and the absolute level of prices that will eventually prevail after controls have been removed. Pegging the exchange rate against a major international currency or basket of currencies—together with liberalized international trade and price stability abroad—allows stable prices to be imported from world markets, and therefore removes this uncertainty to a considerable degree, at least in the case of internationally traded goods. This guideline function of the exchange rate is even more important for those countries with a history of more centralized planning and less flexible prices.

---

[17]However, unless all countries fix their exchange rates, a fixed rate relative to one currency or basket of currencies implies flexibility relative to others.

[18]For a review of optimal exchange rate regime choice, see Aghevli, Khan, and Montiel (1991).

A Currency Board

A currency board represents a limiting case of a permanently pegged exchange rate system, in which the ability of the monetary authorities to increase the domestic money supply is limited by the quantity of their foreign exchange holdings. The currency board stands ready to exchange domestic currency for foreign currency at a fixed rate (plus or minus a margin for transaction costs). The commitment to provide foreign currency typically extends only to domestic currency and not to bank deposits, and the board is obliged to hold realizable financial assets in the foreign currency equal to or greater than the amount of domestic currency outstanding.[19] It functions, therefore, in much the same way as a gold standard, in which domestic currency is backed by gold reserves. Currency boards were established in several British colonies; Hong Kong still operates a currency board based on the U.S. dollar.

The main advantages of a currency board (or a gold-backed currency) are that it enhances the credibility of the commitment to price stability (and the ability to achieve it) by tying the hands of the authorities, and, because it does not require a great deal of expertise, that it can easily be set up by countries that want to have their own currencies but have no tradition of central banking (for example, the states of the former U.S.S.R.). The currency board, by holding its reserves in interest-bearing assets, would allow some seigniorage to be earned, in contrast to the case where the foreign currency itself circulates (or reserves are held in gold). The disadvantages are the lack of monetary flexibility (which may not be an important loss if monetary discipline is absent) and, more important, the requirement that foreign exchange reserves be available.

To the extent that the operation of the currency board restricts only the supply of currency, it is consistent with monetary expansion through financial intermediaries. Increases in broader measures of the money supply, therefore, are not directly constrained by the availability of foreign exchange. The growth of the banking system will, moreover, benefit from the stability of the currency; however, the soundness of the banking system may suffer from the limited ability of the currency board to provide lender-of-last-resort facilities.[20]

Implementing Exchange Rate Stability

There are, however, some conditions for maintaining a pegged exchange rate for an extended period that may be particularly difficult for PCPEs to satisfy in the early stages of reform. While governments may recognize the value of fixed or pegged exchange rates and the associated commitment to strict financial discipline, the PCPEs may still not be ready or able to implement that discipline for the following reasons.

First, the minimum level of foreign exchange reserves (or an exchange stabilization fund made available by other countries) needed to defend the exchange rate parity may not exist. Although, in principle, a sufficiently depreciated rate may ensure that the authorities are able to acquire foreign exchange reserves for subsequent use in resisting exchange rate pressures, the appropriate peg may be very hard to determine. Exchange market participants, observing the low level of reserves, may provoke an exchange crisis and exhaust the reserve stock. Moreover, an overdepreciated rate, rather than contributing to price stability, may set in train an inflationary spiral that is difficult to stop. Thus, the credibility of a commitment to low inflation should not be seen as being the same thing as the credibility of an exchange rate peg.[21]

Second, tight financial policies may not be possible before some structural reforms have been fully implemented. A broad budget balance is required to support appropriate monetary conditions, but this may, in turn, require a substantial reform of the tax system, particularly since public investment—especially in areas such as infrastructure and environmental protection—may be given high priority. Such tax reform would inevitably take time to implement. With limited fiscal resources, the authorities may not be able to recapitalize the banking system or state-owned enterprises holding nonperforming loans—the legacy of a period of soft budget constraints. Tight monetary policies might endanger the survival of these banks and enterprises.

Third, a very tight financial policy stance may not be advisable from a macroeconomic point of view in the transitional conditions of many PCPEs. Because inefficient industries stop production much faster than the sectors with newly found comparative advantage can expand, the introduction of market competition has initially resulted in a sharp fall in production and employment. In these circumstances, a tight stance for financial policies might exacerbate the initial decline in economic

---

[19]See Walters (1989). However, in the North Russian currency board, domestic currency was only 75 percent-backed by foreign assets (Spring Rice, 1919).

[20]In colonial currency boards, these functions were provided by the metropolitan central bank (Walters, 1989).

---

[21]Indeed, overdepreciation in order to maintain a peg may signal the authorities' unwillingness to tighten financial policies.

activity and might even precipitate massive bankruptcies because of the weak financial position of enterprises.

A *fourth* difficulty is uncertainty about the equilibrium level of the real exchange rate (and hence also of the nominal rate, given incomplete price flexibility) that derives from the prolonged history of price controls. Even though it is difficult to assess what constitutes an equilibrium level for the real exchange rate of any country, such calculations are particularly perilous for the PCPEs, both because of insufficient data and the absence of any history of market prices. Moreover, such calculations are further complicated by the fact that a large proportion of the international trade of the PCPEs has been administered on the basis of nonconvertible trade arrangements, in particular within the framework of the former CMEA. The estimation of competitiveness vis-à-vis the countries of the former CMEA is not only hard but perhaps not even meaningful to the extent that nonmarket forces are still significant. Hence, the choice of a fixed exchange rate level is subject to a large margin of error.

The rapid structural changes that the PCPEs are undergoing also make it harder for them to select the foreign currency, or the basket of foreign currencies, to which they should peg their domestic currency. Usually, the basket is chosen to comprise the main partner countries, particularly those with a moderate inflation rate. Thus, if the domestic inflation rate is roughly in line with rates prevailing in these partner countries, international competitiveness will not be greatly affected. But for the PCPEs, the structure of international trade can be expected to change rapidly, and hence also the relative importance of the various partner countries.

Implementing a Floating Rate

On the other hand, a floating exchange rate system also presents difficulties for the PCPEs. *First*, there is the risk of high exchange rate volatility as confidence in the success of the stabilization plan fluctuates. This volatility could have adverse effects on domestic production and trade.

Second, with the loss of the exchange rate as a nominal anchor for domestic prices, the need to find another nominal anchor—for instance, the money supply—increases. But the considerable uncertainty as to the functioning of money markets makes it less desirable to have to rely heavily on money as an intermediate target. On the money demand side, there are no firm estimates on which to base monetary policy; history is certainly of no help (given the existence of chronic disequi-

librium), and current financial innovations may be causing money demand to shift.[22] Under such conditions, the exchange rate appears to be a much more reliable anchor.

In any case, the incomplete development of financial markets makes the relationship between indirect control instruments (such as discount facilities and reserve requirements) and monetary targets a very uncertain one. Given severe institutional deficiencies, a system of credit ceilings is likely to be the only effective and readily available instrument of monetary control.[23] Credit ceilings would serve as an additional nominal anchor, strengthening the effectiveness of either the money supply or the exchange rate. However, the experience of industrial countries with credit controls has been that they distort resource allocation, in particular by rationing credit to small firms that do not have access to financial markets for financing.

Finally, the operation of an efficient and deep foreign exchange market may not be technically feasible in the short run, as the development of financial markets in the PCPEs is generally only embryonic. In view of the linkages between different financial operations, some degree of development in other financial markets is necessary to support the operation of a smoothly running foreign exchange market with a floating rate. An often-cited limitation derived from insufficient financial development is the absence of forward markets for foreign exchange where exporters and importers can hedge risks of exchange rate fluctuations. Although the existence of forward exchange markets is highly desirable, in their absence the authorities should avoid pressures to offer forward cover themselves. Otherwise, they will create incentives against allowing the exchange rate to respond flexibly to economic shocks in order to avoid making losses on their forward positions.

Dual Exchange Rates

A common feature of the liberalization phase has been to postpone liberalization of capital account transactions. That is, whereas foreign exchange is freely available for most current account transactions, access for any other purpose is restricted, and export proceeds must be surrendered for domestic currency. These restrictions on international capital movements are equivalent to a dual exchange rate regime in the sense that there

---

[22]However, under a fixed rate system, shifts in money demand may also cause problems if reserve levels are low.

[23]For a discussion of the financial sector of the PCPEs, see Part I.

is some implicit exchange rate—a "shadow" exchange rate— that would induce market participants to effect precisely those operations that the restrictions permit.[24] The exchange rate duality becomes more transparent when parallel markets for foreign exchange appear, which has almost always been the case in market economies when severe restrictions persist for long enough.[25]

Although a dual exchange rate system is certainly distortionary, its temporary application has been justified in the context of stabilization plans (Kiguel and Liviatan, 1992). The objective is to insulate the economy from the sharp capital movements that may take place in these circumstances— for example, a sudden outflow of capital owing to lack of confidence in the economy.

It is important to remember, however, that the degree of insulation provided by restrictions on foreign exchange transactions (or by a dual exchange rate system) is limited. Eventually, if the discrepancy between the two rates becomes large, leakages develop between the two markets because there is a strong incentive for exporters to try to channel some of their receipts to the parallel market. The experience in developing countries shows that when a large discrepancy develops between the official and parallel rates, the official rate eventually becomes unsustainable.

In addition, there is potentially another kind of exchange rate duality implicit in trade transactions in the PCPEs. This possibility arises from bilateral trade arrangements still in effect with a number of countries and also from trade relations with the states of the former U.S.S.R., because the prices of goods involved in such trade may differ from free market prices. In trade among former CMEA members, for example, prices of goods are, in principle, determined in accordance with world prices, but, for manufactures especially, there can be considerable ambiguity as to what the relevant international price is. In particular, some manufactured goods may not measure up to the quality standards that prevail in Western markets. Nonetheless, if

exporters receive international prices, they will then implicitly benefit from incentives similar to those provided by a preferential exchange rate. Issues associated with trade among former CMEA countries are discussed further in Section IV below.

Conclusions

On balance, the advantages of exchange rate fixity in contributing to stabilization and to shortening the search for market-clearing prices are more important at the initial stage of reform, which is dominated by the effects of price liberalization. If reserves are adequate, or external support in the form of a stabilization fund is available, then pegging the exchange rate may be desirable, subject, however, to the caveat that the choice of the correct level at which to peg is uncertain, and an over-depreciated rate (perhaps chosen to ensure that reserves are sufficient to maintain the peg for an extended period) may exacerbate inflationary pressures.

Once stability is attained—or rather the risk of runaway inflation has been dispelled—other factors that benefit from exchange rate flexibility may become more important. While the completion of structural reforms in the fiscal, monetary, and enterprise areas is indispensable to the functioning of the economy under any exchange rate system, prolonged maintenance of a fixed peg does generally impose more stringent requirements on financial policies. Until structural reforms are completed, it may be very hard to maintain—in the face of limited credibility—the policy stance needed to support an exchange rate peg that was chosen under conditions of great uncertainty. Ultimately, after the reform process has borne fruit, the exchange rate choices of the PCPEs are likely to be dictated by the same criteria as apply to market economies; for instance, some Eastern European countries may want to peg to the European Currency Unit (ECU) in the context of closer economic integration with Western Europe.

Absence of reserves may preclude the option of pegging the exchange rate. Therefore, some degree of flexibility may have to be accepted in any case. Dual exchange rates, although they seem to combine the advantages of pegged and floating rates, are difficult to administer and induce distortions in the allocation of foreign exchange.

---

[24]The problem is somewhat more complicated because access to foreign exchange may be unequal for different enterprises, or different agents, so that the shadow exchange rate that each one of them faces is different.

[25]Dual (or multiple) exchange rates have also been applied to current account transactions when full access to foreign exchange for current account purposes has not been allowed.

IV   The Experience of Eastern European Countries

This section reviews the experience with exchange arrangements of five Eastern European countries—Bulgaria, Czechoslovakia, Hungary, Poland, and Romania—that initiated extensive market-oriented reforms in 1990–91.[26] Discussion of proposals for a multilateral payments system among Eastern European countries to replace the former CMEA created a consensus against such a mechanism, mainly because existing trade was small (except with the former U.S.S.R.) and because such an arrangement would discriminate against trade with market economies.[27] Instead, all five countries have by now established a fairly generalized current account convertibility, either in a "big bang" fashion or in a gradual but still quite speedy way, and have continued to liberalize remaining restrictions. However, the degree of flexibility of the exchange rate systems has varied across countries and over time, ranging from pegged exchange rates to fairly cleanly floating exchange rates. While trade liberalization has generally supported the achievement of balance of payments objectives and the expansion of trade with market economies, trade between Eastern European members of the former CMEA and the former U.S.S.R. collapsed in 1991. Among the reasons for this collapse were difficulties in carrying out trade under hard currency settlements.

Convertibility

The reforming economies of Eastern Europe acted very quickly to remove restrictions on access to foreign exchange for current account transactions.[28] In contrast, access to foreign exchange for capital account transactions—such as acquiring foreign assets—remains very restricted, and exporters are required to surrender their foreign exchange earnings to prevent them from increasing theirm holdings of foreign assets in that way. Bulgaria,[29] Czechoslovakia, and Poland instituted this version of current account convertibility in a "big bang" fashion in conjunction with the liberalization of domestic prices. Hungary and Romania took about one year from the time of substantial domestic price liberalization to remove licensing and other requirements (including limited access to the official market in Romania) for most imports.

While, from an institutional point of view, the PCPEs could be considered not mature enough to support current account convertibility, some crude policy instruments were used to sidestep the institutional deficiencies. Because undeveloped financial markets precluded the use of indirect instruments—such as reserve requirements or a discount window—direct ceilings were imposed on commercial bank credit. Wage controls were instituted to reinforce monetary stringency and prevent a decapitalization of enterprises. Regarding fiscal policy, little flexibility exists until tax reform is implemented; however, an initial windfall gain in profit tax collection generally occurred, which provided considerable initial respite. This windfall gain resulted from the price "jump" at the outset of the reform program, which sharply increased accounting—but generally not economic—profits for enterprises.

Moreover, most PCPEs adopted current account convertibility with only a precarious level of international reserves, typically equivalent to a mere one month of (convertible currency) imports.[30] Although access to international financial markets and to official financial support varied, there was little margin to withstand negative balance of pay-

---

[26]This section was drafted in early 1992 and covers developments until that time, that is, the first one or two years of reform in this group of Eastern European countries.

[27]See, for instance, Kenen (1991) and Polak (1991).

[28]The removal of restrictions was certainly not complete; for example, residents leaving the country for tourism are usually granted granted very limited access to foreign exchange.

[29]The surrender requirement does not apply in Bulgaria, where exporters can hold foreign currency-denominated deposits at domestic banks.

[30]Poland was an exception: it had reserves equivalent to about 3 1/2 months of imports, as well as a stabilization fund that was financed externally.

ment shocks. Therefore, it was feared that a surge in imports—stemming from consumers' appetite for Western goods that had been unavailable for decades—could jeopardize current account convertibility even if generally sound policies were followed. However, after convertibility, imports from non-CMEA countries either declined or were at least roughly matched by the increase in exports to those countries (Table 1). To some extent, this was a reflection of tight financial policies and a competitive exchange rate, but it was also related to the decrease in income experienced at the beginning of the reform process. It still remains to be seen, therefore, whether, as income recovers and access to international financial markets strengthens, an excessive switch of spending toward imported goods will jeopardize the maintenance of current account convertibility.

All five countries, however, maintain restrictions on capital account convertibility at this stage of the reform process, mainly owing to concerns that speculative capital movements might disrupt foreign exchange markets and international trade. Restrictions include unavailability of foreign exchange in the official market for the acquisition of foreign assets by enterprises and households; a surrender requirement for exporters; and restrictions on holdings of foreign assets by enterprises. However, there is little evidence at this stage that restrictions on capital outflows are actually binding; the small—and generally shrinking—premiums on black markets seem to indicate no widespread desire on the part of residents to obtain foreign exchange for purposes other than those allowed under current account convertibility. Adequate returns on domestic assets, credible exchange rate policies, broadening domestic investment opportunities created by privatization, and the expanded availability of imported goods through legal channels are the main reasons for the absence of any generalized tendency toward capital outflows, but the generally shrinking stock of private assets (in real terms) may also have contributed. While, ex post, the small parallel market premiums may indicate that capital controls were unnecessary, they also indicate that the restrictions probably did not create large distortions affecting private (including enterprise) economic decisions. Moreover, by removing the threat of a sudden speculative attack, capital account restrictions may have supported stability in foreign exchange and financial markets.

Exchange Arrangements and Domestic Stabilization

The exchange rate arrangements applied by the countries of Eastern Europe since their economic

reforms started in earnest in 1990–91 cover a broad spectrum: they comprise pegged exchange rates (in Czechoslovakia and, initially, in Poland), a pre-announced crawling peg (in Poland since October 1991), an adjustable crawling peg (in Hungary), a floating exchange rate system (in Bulgaria and, since November 1991, in Romania), and a dual exchange rate system with one fixed and one floating rate (in Romania, initially).

Czechoslovakia and Poland pegged their exchange rates—after very substantial depreciations—at the same time as they implemented major price liberalizations, removed most price subsidies, and substantially adjusted administratively set prices. Although these measures were expected to generate a large increase in the general level of prices on impact, it was considered essential that this price jump not be allowed to put in motion a process of runaway inflation. In both countries, the role of a stable exchange rate as a nominal anchor for prices and in fostering confidence in financial markets was believed crucial at this initial stage of reform.

The policy of using the exchange rate as a nominal anchor seems to have generally supported domestic price stabilization in the two countries. In Poland, inflation, although still relatively high, has fallen considerably (converging to the range of 2–3 percent a month only in the second half of 1991), while in Czechoslovakia—although it might still be too early to judge—inflation appears to be heading to a level similar to that in industrial countries.

A pegged exchange rate regime requires an adequate level of international reserves to cushion against volatility in foreign exchange transactions. Poland's reserve position was boosted by a stabilization fund facility that could be drawn upon if necessary. The stabilization fund, which amounted to $1.0 billion—equivalent to roughly 1.2 months of imports of goods and nonfactor services—was, in fact, never drawn upon. In Czechoslovakia, initial international reserves were very precarious at just over one month of imports at the end of 1990. There was, however, some external financial support—in addition to that provided by the IMF and the World Bank—in the form of balance of payments financing from the Commission of the European Communities and the Group of 24.

The nominal anchor strategy is not, however, without trade-offs. While a more depreciated exchange rate can be expected to be held for longer and to grant, at least initially, higher credibility, it also brings about a larger price increase on impact. In fact, the exchange rate depreciation—together with the increases in administered prices, many of which are directly related to the exchange rate—was one of the major determinants of the price

Table 1. Eastern Europe: Trade with CMEA and Non-CMEA Areas

(Millions of U.S. dollars)

	1989	1990	1991
Bulgaria			
Exports:			
Non-CMEA	3,138	2,615	1,817
CMEA	7,953	5,843	2,070
Total	11,091	8,458	3,887
Imports:			
Non-CMEA	4,337	3,372	2,007
CMEA	9,104	4,554	1,845
Total	13,441	8,031	3,852
Balance:			
Non-CMEA	−1,199	−757	−190
CMEA	−1,151	1,289	225
Total	−2,350	427	35
Czechoslovakia			
Exports:			
Non-CMEA	6,476	6,531	7,120
CMEA	7,735	5,207	3,080
Total	14,211	11,738	10,200
Imports:			
Non-CMEA	6,217	7,345	6,740
CMEA	7,848	5,892	4,160
Total	14,065	13,237	10,900
Balance:			
Non-CMEA	259	−814	380
CMEA	−113	−685	−1,080
Total	146	−1,499	−700
Hungary			
Exports			
Non-CMEA	5,628	6,501	7,412
CMEA	4,045	3,049	1,749
Total	9,673	9,550	9,161
Imports:			
Non-CMEA	5,352	5,691	7,343
CMEA	3,512	2,930	2,681
Total	8,864	8,621	10,024
Balance:			
Non-CMEA	276	810	69
CMA	533	119	−932
Total	809	929	−863
Poland			
Exports:			
Non-CMEA	7,575	11,257	11,146
CMEA	538	3,757	2,063
Total	8,113	15,014	13,209
Imports:			
Non-CMEA	7,335	8,839	10,677
CMEA	652	2,086	2,136
Total	7,987	10,925	12,813
Balance:			
Non-CMEA	240	2,418	469
CMEA	−114	1,671	−73
Total	126	4,089	396
Romania[1]			
Exports:			
Non-CMEA	5,726	3,231	1,939
CMEA	4,761	2,539	921
Total	10,487	5,770	2,860
Imports:			
Non-CMEA	3,299	4,703	2,862
CMEA	5,138	4,411	1,322
Total	8,437	9,114	4,184
Balance:			
Non-CMEA	2,427	−1,472	−923
CMEA	−377	−1,872	−401
Total	2,050	−3,344	−1,324

Source: IMF staff estimates.

[1]Data for 1991 are for January–September only.

jump that took place with the price liberalization. Moreover, it has been argued that the resulting large increase in production costs, together with the tight stance of monetary policy, generated a negative "supply-side" shock to the economy that may account, to a large extent, for the output fall experienced since the launching of the reform program (Calvo and Coricelli, 1992).

But the level at which the authorities decide to peg the exchange rate is not entirely a free parameter in that it is closely related to the general stance of financial policies. If fiscal and monetary policies are tight, there is less need for a large initial depreciation to defend the fixed exchange rate, and thus the price jump can be minimized. If fiscal and monetary policies are not sufficiently tight, an initial overdepreciation may be necessary to make the system less vulnerable to unfavorable shocks, in the expectation that maintaining the exchange rate peg for longer can make a lasting contribution to stabilization. In Poland, the exchange rate was pegged at a level considered sustainable for "a few months" (Lane, 1991). This level, which was, in fact, more depreciated than the parallel market rate,[31] permitted a large increase in exports in 1990 and was sustained for nearly one and a half years. In Czechoslovakia, despite preferring to err on the side of overdepreciation in view of the considerable uncertainty (Aghevli, Borensztein, and van der Willigen, 1992), the authorities pegged the exchange rate at a substantially more appreciated level than that which prevailed in the parallel market; nevertheless, the parallel rate gradually converged to the official rate.

While a loosening of policies in the second half of 1990 set back the stabilization effort in Poland to some extent, the different degree of success in price stabilization in Czechoslovakia and Poland may also be attributable to their different starting positions. Poland, with a history of serious distortions, was already experiencing a mix of massive shortages and hyperinflation in the second half of 1989, and the price jump in January 1990 exceeded 100 percent.[32] By contrast, Czechoslovakia, with a history of moderate shortages and disequilibria, experienced a price jump of only about 50 percent, despite a much broader price liberalization. The experience of other countries that have overcome relatively long periods of very high inflation has shown that a residual inflation comparable to that

---

[31]See Kolodko (1991).

[32]According to Lipton and Sachs (1990), when measured from the beginning to the end of the month, the price increase in January 1990 in Poland was 110 percent. The increase in the consumer price index—which measures the average level of prices over the month—was just under 80 percent.

in Poland is very difficult to eliminate. Chile, Israel, and Mexico, for example, are generally considered to apply broadly appropriate economic policies, but their annual inflation remains in the 20–30 percent range.[33] Measured against that standard, the effects of the stabilization effort on inflation in Poland are not atypical.

Exchange Arrangements and International Competitiveness

Notwithstanding the nominal anchor function, exchange rate policy has its most direct effect on the balance of payments position. In May 1991, after nearly one and a half years of imposing a pegged rate, Poland depreciated the exchange rate parity in response to the appreciation of the U.S. dollar (to which the zloty was pegged) and to the drop in exports to other former CMEA countries. Competitiveness had deteriorated considerably from the level of January 1990. Poland also broadened the peg from the U.S. dollar alone to a basket comprising the currencies of its main trading partners. Some five months later, in October 1991, facing a moderate but persistent deterioration in competitiveness and a less favorable economic outlook, Poland again changed the exchange rate regime to a preannounced crawling peg, that is, a preannounced schedule of monthly depreciation rates of the zloty vis-à-vis the basket of currencies.

Czechoslovakia has made a firmer commitment to maintaining the fixed exchange rate regime. On the one hand, domestic inflation has subsided considerably and can be expected to converge to levels comparable to those countries to whose currencies the exchange rate is pegged. On the other hand, the general policy stance and the orientation of the Government seem more compatible with maintaining a fixed exchange rate. However, it may be premature to draw a sharp distinction between the two countries because Czechoslovakia implemented current account convertibility at a fixed exchange rate on January 1, 1991, exactly a year later than did Poland.

In adopting the preannounced crawling peg system in October 1991, Poland essentially adapted a fixed exchange rate regime to a situation in which it

was recognized that domestic inflation would persistently exceed that in partner countries. The predetermined schedule of daily depreciations precludes any surprise change in the exchange rate.[34] Although not a stated policy intention, the depreciation rates are gradually decreasing in percentage terms, which is consistent with a gradual convergence of inflation to international levels. This system does not, however, appear to be the best suited to recover losses in competitiveness, particularly when inflation expectations appear stubborn, and the commitment of the authorities to impose the necessary financial discipline is not assured.[35] The most similar alternative policy—a fixed exchange rate after an initial depreciation to correct the loss of competitiveness, plus a cushion for further expected losses—would offer the advantage of boosting competitiveness up front and of enhancing credibility. A higher initial inflation rate would also follow, but chances of subsequent stabilization would improve.

Despite the parallels in their exchange arrangements, Poland's external position was boosted more than that of Czechoslovakia. In 1990, Polish exports to non-CMEA markets increased by nearly 50 percent (in current dollars), and they are estimated to have remained stationary in 1991, notwithstanding the appreciation in the real exchange rate. In Czechoslovakia, exports to non-CMEA markets are estimated to have grown by a more modest 9 percent (in current dollars) in 1991, the first year of market liberalization (Table 1). This more moderate increase may have several causes. *First*, the very limited enterprise autonomy before liberalization in Czechoslovakia, including dependence on the now-dismantled foreign trade organizations for all international trade-related activities, may account for a slower or less complete response to market incentives. *Second*, the structure of production, which includes armaments, machinery, and relatively high technology manufactures, may make it more difficult for Czechoslovakia to find markets in Western economies without substantial restructuring of production and commercialization. And, *third*, despite the substantial nominal depreciation and wage restraint policy, increases in raw material and energy prices—owing in part to the change in pricing policies in the former CMEA discussed below—may imply that actual gains in competitiveness were smaller than those in Poland.

---

[33]An investigation of the reasons for the stubbornness of residual inflation goes beyond the scope of this paper; however, the phenomenon is quite generalized and may be partly explained by lack of full credibility and increasing costs of adjustment. See Agénor and Taylor (1992) and Calvo and Végh (1991). Alternatively, pursuing a real exchange rate target may also lead to a stable but high rate of inflation under some circumstances. See Montiel and Ostry (1991).

[34]There is, however, no explicit commitment as to how long this exchange rate policy will be continued.

[35]The application of a preannounced schedule of exchange rate depreciation in the Southern Cone of Latin America in the early 1980s and, more recently, in Mexico, generated real appreciation of the exchange rate. See Calvo and Végh (1991).

In fact, it is very difficult to assess real exchange rate developments in the five Eastern European countries because of the lack of a meaningful benchmark given the history of price controls and distortions. Chart 1 nevertheless presents the recent evolution of the nominal exchange rate (vis-à-vis the U.S. dollar), and Chart 2 displays monthly rates of inflation.

Whereas Czechoslovakia and Poland have given price stabilization higher priority, the other PCPEs have given greater weight to achieving a comfortable balance of payments position in choosing their exchange arrangements. The adjustable peg system adopted by *Hungary* involves considerably more flexibility; the exchange rate can be adjusted unexpectedly and has been devalued on two occasions to defend the competitiveness of the forint. Hungary's greater concern for balance of payments considerations appears justified by the objective of avoiding a rescheduling of foreign debt, which would be undermined by a deterioration of the external current account, and by a relatively smoother transition to domestic price liberalization than in the other PCPEs. With about 50 percent of domestic prices already freed by 1988, Hungary did not face the same magnitude of market disequilibria as did Poland or even Czechoslovakia. It could, therefore, afford to undertake a more gradual market liberalization, one that would not pose a major stabilization challenge.

The exchange rate system chosen by Hungary has, so far, been effective in maintaining external balance. Exports to the traditional convertible currency area have increased by more than 40 percent cumulatively during 1990 and 1991 (in current dollars), debt rescheduling has been avoided, and access to private international financial markets has been maintained despite some downgrading of the bond rating. Inflation, however, remained slightly above an annual rate of 30 percent in 1990–91, partly because of the gradual price liberalization and adjustment of administered prices (Chart 2).

Unlike the other countries, *Bulgaria* adopted a freely floating rate, with relatively limited central bank intervention in the foreign exchange market. Its choice of regime was governed principally by uncertainty about the equilibrium level of the exchange rate together with critically low foreign exchange reserves and lack of access to foreign financing—partly owing to the difficult foreign debt position. Except for a large initial overshooting, the market has not been excessively volatile, with foreign exchange trading in a margin of about 6–8 percent on either side of the lev's average value against the dollar. With an active interest rate policy to support the lev, there has not been strong downward pressure against the currency, and central bank intervention has, in fact, been mostly on the side of buying foreign exchange. The level at which the exchange rate stabilized is still substantially more depreciated than it was before floating started and price liberalization was enacted in February 1991 (Chart 1), and, although precise unit labor cost data are not available, the real exchange rate is widely believed to be still very competitive despite its considerable appreciation since floating started.

Despite the apparently adequate level of competitiveness during 1991, Bulgarian exports to non-CMEA markets fell sharply relative to 1990 largely because of shortages of oil and oil products owing to disruptions in trade with the former U.S.S.R. and to difficulties in obtaining external trade financing. In addition, in view of their very limited experience under market conditions and the high investment needed to transform their distorted production structure, enterprises have not been very successful in redirecting and expanding production for export markets. Inflation, moreover, has not been easy to control, although the floating exchange rate system, while it does not provide a nominal anchor, does not appear to have aggravated the price spiral.

Romania initially adopted a dual exchange rate system, but one in which a floating interbank market played a substantial role. An official exchange rate, at which 50 percent of most export proceeds had to be surrendered and at which imports of raw materials for industrial use were available in limited quantities, operated side by side with a freely floating interbank rate at which current account transactions could be carried out virtually without restriction. The reluctance of the authorities to move directly to a unified floating rate with full current account convertibility originated in fears of excessive volatility in this market, particularly in view of the inexperience of enterprises in dealing with flexible prices in general, and a level of reserves that was deemed too low to allow significant official intervention in foreign exchange markets.

The policy of applying an appreciated official rate to a portion of trade limited the price jumps that followed the partial price liberalizations implemented in November 1990, April 1991, and July 1991. The interbank market operated at a substantial premium—about 500 percent of the official rate initially and some 200 percent later—following a devaluation of the official rate and an appreciation of the free rate. Significant leakages between the two markets subsequently emerged. The feared excess volatility of the foreign exchange market did

Chart 1. Eastern Europe: Exchange Rates
(End of period: log scale)

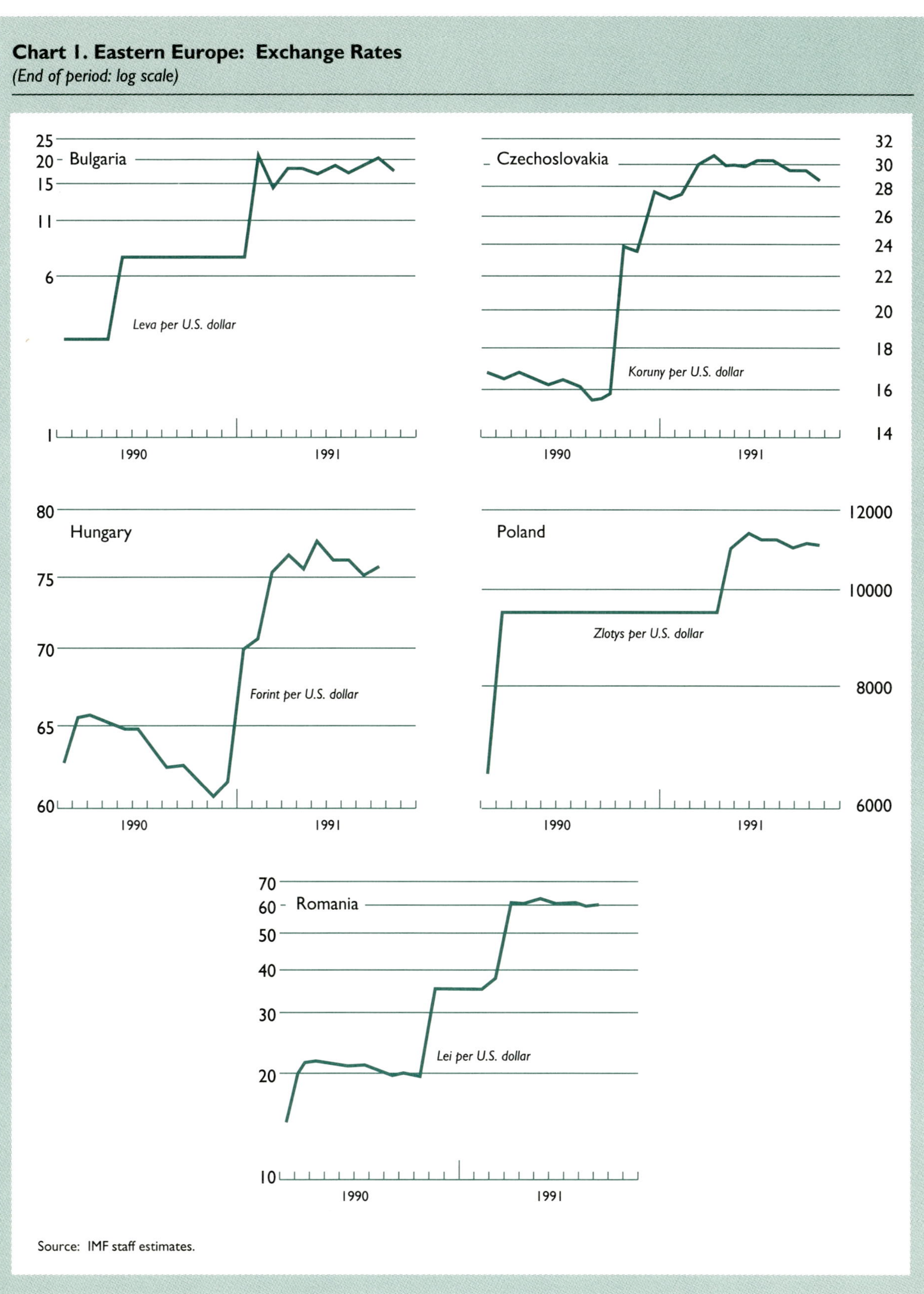

Source: IMF staff estimates.

Chart 2. Eastern Europe: CPI Inflation Rates
(Monthly percentage change)

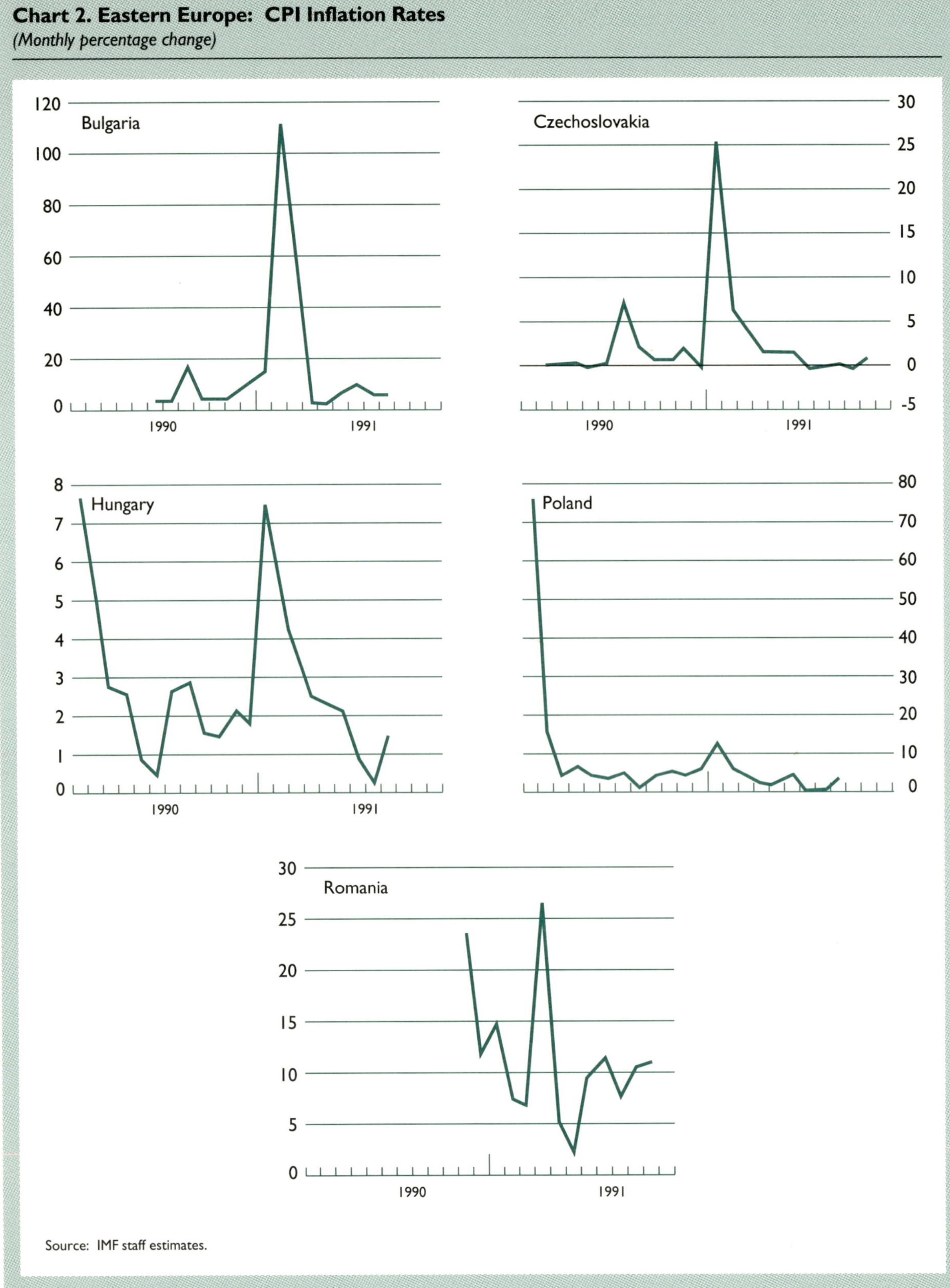

Source: IMF staff estimates.

not materialize, and the market expanded further as new smaller intermediaries, such as travel agencies and foreign exchange bureaus, were authorized to participate. In November 1991, the two markets were finally unified and most restrictions lifted, with the authorities pursuing a managed float policy to support the very significant depreciation of the real exchange rate that occurred after the onset of the reform program.

While the dual system makes it even harder to assess the degree of competitiveness afforded by the exchange rate, the fall in Romania's exports to non-CMEA markets cannot be explained solely by exchange rate developments. Most of that fall was concentrated in petroleum products, whose production declined owing to inadequate financing for imports of crude oil, which now required convertible currency settlement. Moreover, domestic supply problems, including those arising from breakdowns in the payments system, which was related to the inter-enterprise arrears situation, also contributed to the weak export performance. As in Bulgaria, even after accounting for the impact of price liberalization, the inflation rate in Romania remained high, at an average underlying rate of 7–8 percent a month.

CMEA Trade and Payments

While exchange rate policies have played a generally favorable role in fostering exports to convertible currency areas, they have not offset the collapse of exports to the CMEA area that followed its dismantling on January 1, 1991. Trade among CMEA member countries previously accounted for a high proportion of the total trade of these countries, in particular, trade between the U.S.S.R. and the East European CMEA countries (Table 2). Within the Eastern European bloc, however, the degree of dependence on CMEA trade, particularly trade with the U.S.S.R., differed significantly. In 1989, for example, over 57 percent of Bulgaria's exports went to the CMEA area, and nearly 50 percent went to the U.S.S.R. Romania, at the other extreme, sent only 20 percent of its exports to CMEA countries and a little less than 14 percent to the U.S.S.R. (Table 2).

Two aspects of the CMEA trade regime were particularly damaging to the PCPEs. The first was the underlying pattern of trade and its concentration in foreign trade organizations, which meant that producers did not find it necessary to develop a marketing infrastructure for exports. Guaranteed exports under the umbrella of bilateral treaties undermined incentives for enterprises to improve the quality of manufactured goods. Bilateral trade planning—in the context of protocols that fixed the quantities and prices of the products to be traded—imposed limitations on a country's ability to adapt the structure of its exports to shifts in the composition of world demand.

The second aspect concerned access to low-cost imports of raw materials from the former U.S.S.R. While this shielded CMEA economies from exogenous shocks, it had several undesirable side effects, including promoting energy inefficiency and maintaining energy-intensive industrial activity with uncertain prospects in non-CMEA markets. With a move to world prices for energy products in 1991, industrial enterprises often faced costs for imports at world prices higher than the corresponding world market value of the goods produced.

The CMEA countries agreed, at their 1990 meeting in Sofia, to trade with one another in convertible currencies and at world market prices beginning in January 1991; the CMEA itself was, however, subsequently disbanded. A collapse in the volume of trade ensued in 1991 (Table 3). Whereas this trade contraction to some extent resulted from the inefficiency of CMEA trade flows arranged under central planning and from the decline in the level of economic activity in both Eastern Europe and the former Soviet Union, the agreed change in rules was also an obstacle to the continuation of trade flows, in view of a scarcity of reserves and of foreign trade financing.

Eastern Europe quickly moved to freely determined prices and to current account convertibility, but access to foreign exchange in the former U.S.S.R. was seriously rationed and was simply unavailable for many importing enterprises in the states of the former Soviet Union. However, since the trade collapse, bilateral trade agreements have been made between the Eastern European PCPEs and the Soviet Union, and, more recently, with the states of the former U.S.S.R. individually. Agreements that have been concluded or are in the process of negotiation include "indicative lists" of tradable goods with some kind of clearing arrangement (with settlement generally in hard currency), clearing arrangements with settlement in domestic currencies, and barter deals. These arrangements have allowed some recovery in exports to the former Soviet Union, and the actual decline in trade in 1991 was not as dramatic as initially feared.

Lessons from the Eastern European Experience

Although the PCPEs have limited control over economic policy instruments, and state enterprises do not respond to market incentives as quickly as

Table 2. Eastern Europe and the U.S.S.R.: Shares of Exports to Former CMEA Countries in Total Exports, 1989

(In percent)

			Importer					
Exporter	Bulgaria	Czechoslovakia	Hungary	Poland	Romania	U.S.S.R.	Total CMEA	Total Non-CMEA
Bulgaria	—	3.3	1.0	2.7	1.5	48.8	57.3	42.7
Czechoslovakia	2.0	—	3.6	7.1	1.6	26.5	40.9	59.1
Hungary	0.7	5.3	—	2.9	1.5	25.4	35.8	64.2
Poland	1.9	7.0	2.2	—	1.3	27.2	39.7	60.3
Romania	1.0	1.9	1.6	1.8	—	13.6	19.9	80.1
U.S.S.R.	12.8	14.3	9.3	12.7	6.1	—	55.3	44.7

Source: Kenen, Peter B., "Transitional Arrangements for Trade and Payments Among the CMEA Countries," *Staff Papers*, International Monetary Fund, Vol. 38 (June 1991), Tables 2 and 3. The calculation of these shares is sensitive to the exchange rate used for the transferable ruble, which is assumed here to be $0.50/ruble.

Table 3. Eastern Europe: Annual Changes in the Volume of Exports, 1991

(In percent)

	To Ex-CMEA	Of Which: U.S.S.R.	To Convertible Currency Area[1]
Bulgaria	−64	−57	−30
Czechoslovakia	−68	−63	−11
Hungary	−67	−69	15
Poland	−71	−74	−1
Romania	−60	−60	−33

Sources: National authorities and IMF staff estimates.

[1]Excluding convertible currency exports to former CMEA countries.

could be desired, Eastern European countries have been able to institute current account convertibility. Because of undeveloped markets, some crude policy instruments—such as wage controls and ceilings on bank credit—have had to be used instead of the normally more efficient indirect instruments. But with the aid of those instruments, current account convertibility has been possible, and, with it, the external sector has played an important role in providing competition and market incentives for domestic firms as well as enlarged consumption opportunities.

The experiences of Czechoslovakia and Poland indicate that a pegged exchange rate regime can be credible and can contribute to domestic price stabilization in the initial phase of price liberalization. Accompanied by trade liberalization, the pegged exchange rate served not only as a nominal anchor for the level of domestic prices but also as a guideline enabling individual market-clearing prices to be achieved quickly across a range of tradable goods. However, a large initial depreciation—required to hold the pegged rate for a sufficiently long period—implied a larger price jump on impact, which could create a supply-side output contraction and run the risk of setting in motion an inflationary spiral. If financial policies are sufficiently tight, the required initial depreciation is much smaller.

While, ultimately, disciplined and credible financial policies are the basis for both price stability and external balance under any exchange rate system, a pegged exchange rate can make an important contribution to stabilization during a massive price liberalization. This requires, however, a sufficiently high level of foreign reserves or external support, in the absence of which greater exchange rate flexibility may be inevitable. A pegged exchange rate should not, moreover, be maintained for too long in circumstances in which the economy cannot fairly quickly achieve an inflation rate commensurate with that of its trading partners. More flexible exchange rate systems have been operated successfully in several countries despite rudimentary financial sectors.

As concerns trade with other former CMEA members, the unequal pace of economic reform and the shortage of hard currency have become serious obstacles to maintaining trade flows that are otherwise justified by comparative advantage. This situation may be reproduced among the states of the former Soviet Union that abandon a common currency and attempt to settle trade in convertible currencies. Bilateral clearing agreements are being used to re-establish trade between the states of the former U.S.S.R. and the Eastern European PCPEs, although the large number required and the distortions that they may introduce underline the advantages of a multilateral payments system.

V Summary and Conclusions

From the albeit brief reform experience of Eastern Europe, a number of tentative conclusions can be drawn concerning exchange arrangements for the PCPEs, at least in the early stages of reform.

Generally, the rapid move to current account convertibility in the countries of Eastern Europe—in particular, Bulgaria, Czechoslovakia, Hungary, Poland, and Romania—has been accomplished successfully despite rudimentary financial markets and shortages of reserves. The discipline of foreign competition and guidelines from foreign prices have made a notable contribution to reform. Convertibility has, however, been accompanied by initial overdepreciation in several countries.

Various restrictions still remain on capital account transactions. It seems that capital account convertibility might best be postponed until the economy is strong enough to resist potential speculative attacks. However, full convertibility minimizes distortions in the allocation of resources and enhances monetary discipline and, hence, should be considered a medium-term objective. In any case, a degree of de facto capital account convertibility will prevail despite the existence of restrictions.

A fixed exchange rate may be an especially useful anchor in the initial stages of liberalization to the extent that it helps achieve stabilization and prevents the price jump from provoking a self-reinforcing inflation process. However, there is a danger that an initial overdepreciation may add to inflationary pressures. The exchange rate commitment also requires adequate foreign exchange reserves to be feasible.

After an initial phase, a pegged exchange rate may be difficult to maintain, given weak policy institutions, pressures for government spending, and uncertainty about the correct rate in the context of major transformations of the economy. More flexible arrangements that have been operated without generating excessive volatility are a floating exchange rate (Bulgaria and Romania) and an adjustable, or crawling, peg (Hungary and, since October 1991, Poland).

In view of the interdependence of the PCPEs, the negative effects on economic activity of the breakdown of trade among them are very serious. Low foreign exchange reserves, distrust among trading partners, and lack of trade credit may justify implementing transitional arrangements that fall short of generalized convertibility, perhaps with the aid of an outside institution to provide initial capital and administration. Current account convertibility with all trading partners, if feasible, is, however, the surest guarantee that the benefits of international competition will get translated into the process of reform and that trade among the PCPEs will reflect comparative advantage.

References

Agénor, Pierre-Richard, and Mark P. Taylor, "Testing for Credibility Effects," *Staff Papers*, International Monetary Fund, Vol. 39 (September 1992), pp. 545–71.

Aghevli, Bijan, Eduardo Borensztein, and Tessa van der Willigen, *Stabilization and Structural Reform in the Czech and Slovak Federal Republic: First Stage*, Occasional Paper 92 (Washington: International Monetary Fund, March 1992).

Aghevli, Bijan, Mohsin Khan, and Peter Montiel, *Exchange Rate Policy in Developing Countries: Some Analytical Issues*, Occasional Paper 78 (Washington: International Monetary Fund, 1991).

Akerlof, George, and others, "East Germany in from the Cold: The Economic Aftermath of Currency Union," *Brookings Papers on Economic Activity: 1* (Washington: The Brookings Institution, 1991).

Calvo, Guillermo A., and Jacob A. Frenkel, "Credit Markets, Credibility, and Economic Transformation," *Journal of Economic Perspectives*, Vol. 5 (Fall 1991), pp. 139–48.

Calvo, Guillermo A., and Fabrizio Coricelli, "Stabilizing a Previously Centrally Planned Economy: Poland 1990," *Economic Policy: A European Forum* (April 1992), pp. 176–226.

Calvo, Guillermo A., and Manmohan S. Kumar, "Financial Markets and Intermediation" (Part I of this Occasional Paper).

Dooley, Michael P., "Capital Flight: A Response to Differences in Financial Risks," *Staff Papers*, International Monetary Fund, Vol. 35 (September 1988), pp. 422–36.

Frenkel, Jacob A., Morris Goldstein, and Paul R. Masson, *Characteristics of a Successful Exchange Rate System*, Occasional Paper 82 (Washington: International Monetary Fund, July 1991).

Gilman, Martin G., "Heading for Currency Convertibility," *Finance and Development*, International Monetary Fund and World Bank, Vol. 27 (September 1990), pp. 32–34.

Gold, Joseph, "The Fund's Concepts of Convertibility," IMF Pamphlet Series No. 14 (Washington: International Monetary Fund, 1971).

Greene, Joshua E., and Peter Isard, *Currency Convertibility and the Transformation of Centrally Planned Economies*, Occasional Paper 81 (Washington: International Monetary Fund, June 1991).

Haberler, Gottfried, "Currency Convertibility," National Economic Problems Series No. 451, American Enterprise Association, Washington (1954).

Kaplan, Jacob J., and Gunther Schleiminger, *The European Payments Union: Financial Diplomacy in the 1950s* (Oxford, England: Clarendon Press, 1989).

Kenen, Peter B., "Transitional Arrangements for Trade and Payments Among the CMEA Countries," *Staff Papers*, International Monetary Fund, Vol. 38 (June 1991), pp. 235–67.

Kiguel, Miguel, and Nissan Liviatan, "The Business Cycle Associated with Exchange Rate-Based Stabilizations," *World Bank Economic Review*, Vol. 6 (May 1992), pp. 279–305.

Kolodko, Grzegorz, "Inflation Stabilization in Poland: A Year After," *Rivista di Politica Economica*, Vol. 81 (June 1991), pp. 289–330.

Lane, Timothy, "Inflation Stabilization and Economic Transformation in Poland: The First Year," Carnegie-Rochester Conference Series on Public Policy, Vol. 36 (July 1991).

Lipton, David, and Jeffrey Sachs, "Creating a Market Economy in Eastern Europe: The Case of Poland," *Brookings Papers on Economic Activity: 1* (Washington: The Brookings Institution, 1990), pp. 75–133.

McKinnon, Ronald I., "Liberalizing Foreign Trade in a Socialist Economy," in Williamson (1991b), pp. 96–115.

Montiel, Peter, and Jonathan Ostry, "Macroeconomic Implications of Real Exchange Rate Targeting in Developing Countries," *Staff Papers*, International Monetary Fund, Vol. 38 (December 1991), pp. 872–900.

Nuti, Domenico Mario, "Comment," in Williamson (1991b), pp. 48–55.

Polak, Jacques J., "Currency Convertibility in Eastern Europe: An Indispensable Element in the Transition Process," in Williamson (1991b), pp. 21–47.

Spring Rice, D., "The North Russian Currency," *Economic Journal*, Vol. 29 (September 1919), pp. 280–89.

Walters, Alan, "Currency Boards," in John Eatwell, Murray Milgate, and Peter Newman, eds. *The New Palgrave: Money* (New York: Norton, 1989), pp. 109–14.

Williamson, John (1991a), *The Economic Opening of Eastern Europe* (Washington: Institute for International Economics).

——— (1991b), ed., *Currency Convertibility in Eastern Europe* (Washington: Institute for International Economics).

Recent Occasional Papers of the International Monetary Fund

102. Financial Sector Reforms and Exchange Arrangements in Eastern Europe. Part I: Financial Markets and Intermediation, by Guillermo A. Calvo and Manmohan S. Kumar. Part II: Exchange Arrangements of Previously Centrally Planned Economies, by Eduardo Borensztein and Paul R. Masson. 1993.

101. Spain: Converging with the European Community, by Michel Galy, Gonzalo Pastor, and Thierry Pujol. 1993.

100. The Gambia: Economic Adjustment in a Small Open Economy, by Michael T. Hadjimichael, Thomas Rumbaugh, and Eric Verreydt. 1992.

99. Mexico: The Strategy to Achieve Sustained Economic Growth, edited by Claudio Loser and Eliot Kalter. 1992.

98. Albania: From Isolation Toward Reform, by Mario I. Blejer, Mauro Mecagni, Ratna Sahay, Richard Hides, Barry Johnston, Piroska Nagy, and Roy Pepper. 1992.

97. Rules and Discretion in International Economic Policy, by Manuel Guitián. 1992.

96. Policy Issues in the Evolving International Monetary System, by Morris Goldstein, Peter Isard, Paul R. Masson, and Mark P. Taylor. 1992.

95. The Fiscal Dimensions of Adjustment in Low-Income Countries, by Karim Nashashibi, Sanjeev Gupta, Claire Liuksila, Henri Lorie, and Walter Mahler. 1992.

94. Tax Harmonization in the European Community: Policy Issues and Analysis, edited by George Kopits. 1992.

93. Regional Trade Arrangements, by Augusto de la Torre and Margaret R. Kelly. 1992.

92. Stabilization and Structural Reform in the Czech and Slovak Federal Republic: First Stage, by Bijan B. Aghevli, Eduardo Borensztein, and Tessa van der Willigen. 1992.

91. Economic Policies for a New South Africa, edited by Desmond Lachman and Kenneth Bercuson with a staff team comprising Daudi Ballali, Robert Corker, Charalambos Christofides, and James Wein. 1992.

90. The Internationalization of Currencies: An Appraisal of the Japanese Yen, by George S. Tavlas and Yuzuru Ozeki. 1992.

89. The Romanian Economic Reform Program, by Dimitri G. Demekas and Mohsin S. Khan. 1991.

88. Value-Added Tax: Administrative and Policy Issues, edited by Alan A. Tait. 1991.

87. Financial Assistance from Arab Countries and Arab Regional Institutions, by Pierre van den Boogaerde. 1991.

86. Ghana: Adjustment and Growth, 1983–91, by Ishan Kapur, Michael T. Hadjimichael, Paul Hilbers, Jerald Schiff, and Philippe Szymczak. 1991.

85. Thailand: Adjusting to Success—Current Policy Issues, by David Robinson, Yangho Byeon, and Ranjit Teja with Wanda Tseng. 1991.

84. Financial Liberalization, Money Demand, and Monetary Policy in Asian Countries, by Wanda Tseng and Robert Corker. 1991.

83. Economic Reform in Hungary Since 1968, by Anthony R. Boote and Janos Somogyi. 1991.

82. Characteristics of a Successful Exchange Rate System, by Jacob A. Frenkel, Morris Goldstein, and Paul R. Masson. 1991.

81. Currency Convertibility and the Transformation of Centrally Planned Economies, by Joshua E. Greene and Peter Isard. 1991.

80. Domestic Public Debt of Externally Indebted Countries, by Pablo E. Guidotti and Manmohan S. Kumar. 1991.

79. The Mongolian People's Republic: Toward a Market Economy, by Elizabeth Milne, John Leimone, Franek Rozwadowski, and Padej Sukachevin. 1991.

78. Exchange Rate Policy in Developing Countries: Some Analytical Issues, by Bijan B. Aghevli, Mohsin S. Khan, and Peter J. Montiel. 1991.

77. Determinants and Systemic Consequences of International Capital Flows, by Morris Goldstein, Donald J. Mathieson, David Folkerts-Landau, Timothy Lane, J. Saúl Lizondo, and Liliana Rojas-Suárez. 1991.

76. China: Economic Reform and Macroeconomic Management, by Mario Blejer, David Burton, Steven Dunaway, and Gyorgy Szapary. 1991.

75. German Unification: Economic Issues, edited by Leslie Lipschitz and Donogh McDonald. 1990.

74. The Impact of the European Community's Internal Market on the EFTA, by Richard K. Abrams, Peter K. Cornelius, Per L. Hedfors, and Gunnar Tersman. 1990.

73. The European Monetary System: Developments and Perspectives, by Horst Ungerer, Jouko J. Hauvonen, Augusto Lopez-Claros, and Thomas Mayer. 1990.

72. The Czech and Slovak Federal Republic: An Economy in Transition, by Jim Prust and an IMF Staff Team. 1990.

71. MULTIMOD Mark II: A Revised and Extended Model, by Paul Masson, Steven Symansky, and Guy Meredith. 1990.

70. The Conduct of Monetary Policy in the Major Industrial Countries: Instruments and Operating Procedures, by Dallas S. Batten, Michael P. Blackwell, In-Su Kim, Simon E. Nocera, and Yuzuru Ozeki. 1990.

69. International Comparisons of Government Expenditure Revisited: The Developing Countries, 1975–86, by Peter S. Heller and Jack Diamond. 1990.

68. Debt Reduction and Economic Activity, by Michael P. Dooley, David Folkerts-Landau, Richard D. Haas, Steven A. Symansky, and Ralph W. Tryon. 1990.

67. The Role of National Saving in the World Economy: Recent Trends and Prospects, by Bijan B. Aghevli, James M. Boughton, Peter J. Montiel, Delano Villanueva, and Geoffrey Woglom. 1990.

66. The European Monetary System in the Context of the Integration of European Financial Markets, by David Folkerts-Landau and Donald J. Mathieson. 1989.

65. Managing Financial Risks in Indebted Developing Countries, by Donald J. Mathieson, David Folkerts-Landau, Timothy Lane, and Iqbal Zaidi. 1989.

64. The Federal Republic of Germany: Adjustment in a Surplus Country, by Leslie Lipschitz, Jeroen Kremers, Thomas Mayer, and Donogh McDonald. 1989.

63. Issues and Developments in International Trade Policy, by Margaret Kelly, Naheed Kirmani, Miranda Xafa, Clemens Boonekamp, and Peter Winglee. 1988.

62. The Common Agricultural Policy of the European Community: Principles and Consequences, by Julius Rosenblatt, Thomas Mayer, Kasper Bartholdy, Dimitrios Demekas, Sanjeev Gupta, and Leslie Lipschitz. 1988.

61. Policy Coordination in the European Monetary System. Part I: The European Monetary System: A Balance Between Rules and Discretion, by Manuel Guitián. Part II: Monetary Coordination Within the European Monetary System: Is There a Rule? by Massimo Russo and Giuseppe Tullio. 1988.

60. Policies for Developing Forward Foreign Exchange Markets, by Peter J. Quirk, Graham Hacche, Viktor Schoofs, and Lothar Weniger. 1988.

59. Measurement of Fiscal Impact: Methodological Issues, edited by Mario I. Blejer and Ke-Young Chu. 1988.

58. The Implications of Fund-Supported Adjustment Programs for Poverty: Experiences in Selected Countries, by Peter S. Heller, A. Lans Bovenberg, Thanos Catsambas, Ke-Young Chu, and Parthasarathi Shome. 1988.

Note: For information on the title and availability of Occasional Papers not listed, please consult the IMF *Publications Catalog* or contact IMF Publication Services.